Table of Contents

Introduction

What Is Readers' Theater?

One good way to gain an understanding of readers' theater is to first get a clear picture of what it is *not*. Readers' theater is not a fully-staged production with sets, costumes, and dramatic action performed by actors who memorize lines from a script. Instead, a readers' theater performance is a dramatic reading, just as its name suggests. Readers are usually seated, reading from a script that is held in their hands or placed on a music stand in front of them. There may be minimal use of costumes or props, such as hats, a scepter or crown, or a simple backdrop to provide a suggestion of the setting and characters that the readers hope to bring to life for the audience during their dramatic reading.

Readers' theater offers all the enrichment of traditional theater productions, but without the logistical challenges that come with designing and building sets and creating costumes. Students are spared the stress of having to memorize lines, and can instead focus on developing a strong dramatic reading of the script.

How to Integrate *Readers' Theater* into Your Classroom

The *Readers' Theater* scripts may be used in a variety of settings for a range of educational purposes. Consider the following:

Language Arts blocks are ideal for incorporating *Readers' Theater* scripts, with their emphasis on reading aloud with expression. Many of the follow-up activities that accompany each script address key skills from the reading/language arts curriculum.

Content-Area Instruction can come alive when you use a *Readers' Theater* script to help explore social studies, science, or math concepts. Check the Table of Contents for the grade-level content-area connections in each script.

Integrated Thematic Teaching can continue throughout the day when you use *Readers' Theater* scripts to help you maintain your thematic focus across all areas of the curriculum, from language arts instruction through content-area lessons.

School Assemblies and Holiday Programs provide the perfect opportunity to showcase student performances. Consider presenting a *Readers' Theater* performance for Black History Month, Women's History Month, for parent evenings, or any other occasion when your students are invited to perform.

Teaching the *Readers' Theater* Units

The 15 units in this volume each include the following:

- A **teacher page** to help you plan instruction:

A short **summary** gives you an overview of each script's plot.

Use the **number of parts** to choose the number of readers to assign per role. Or, you may wish to create two or more casts for each production.

Background information provides facts that you may need to know about the subject treated in the script. It also guides you in activating students' prior knowledge or in building background about new or unfamiliar topics. This helps promote success for students as they approach each new script.

A **unit-level table of contents** gives you at-a-glance information on the script and the follow-up activities.

Vocabulary that may be new or unfamiliar to students is called out so that you can introduce it prior to reading the script.

Staging ideas may be included for some scripts. These optional ideas offer quick and easy suggestions to help both readers and their audience connect with the characters and setting of the play.

An **encore** feature for some scripts includes quick, optional ideas to extend learning related to the content of the script. Ideas range from retelling activities and related literature to ideas for other types of performances.

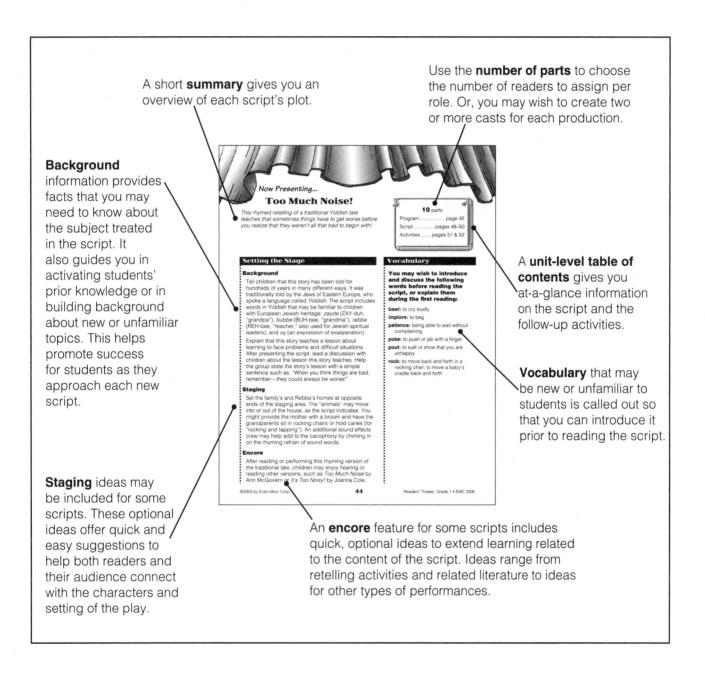

Now Presenting...
Too Much Noise!
This rhymed retelling of a traditional Yiddish tale teaches that sometimes things have to get worse before you realize that they weren't all that bad to begin with!

10 parts
Program.................. page 45
Script ....pages 46–50
Activities ....pages 51 & 52

Setting the Stage

Background

Tell children that this story has been told for hundreds of years in many different ways. It was traditionally told by the Jews of Eastern Europe, who spoke a language called *Yiddish*. The script includes words in Yiddish that may be familiar to children with European Jewish heritage: *zayde* (ZAY-duh, "grandpa"), *bubbe* (BUH-bee, "grandma"), *rebbe* (REH-bee, "teacher," also used for Jewish spiritual leaders), and *oy* (an expression of exasperation).

Explain that this story teaches a lesson about learning to face problems and difficult situations. After presenting the script, lead a discussion with children about the lesson this story teaches. Help the group state the story's lesson with a simple sentence such as, "When you think things are bad, remember—they could always be worse!"

Staging

Set the family's and Rebbe's homes at opposite ends of the staging area. The "animals" may move into or out of the house, as the script indicates. You might provide the mother with a broom and have the grandparents sit in rocking chairs or hold canes (for "rocking and tapping"). An additional sound effects crew may help add to the cacophony by chiming in on the rhyming refrain of sound words.

Encore

After reading or performing this rhyming version of the traditional tale, children may enjoy hearing or reading other versions, such as *Too Much Noise* by Ann McGovern or *It's Too Noisy!* by Joanna Cole.

©2003 by Evan-Moor Corp.

Vocabulary

You may wish to introduce and discuss the following words before reading the script, or explain them during the first reading:

bawl: to cry loudly

implore: to beg

patience: being able to wait without complaining

poke: to push or jab with a finger

pout: to sulk or show that you are unhappy

rock: to move back and forth in a rocking chair; to move a baby's cradle back and forth

44

Readers' Theater, Grade 1 • EMC 3306

- A reproducible **program** page provides an introduction to the script and a list of characters. Use this page to list the names of students who will read each role, and distribute it to your audience to enhance the theater-going experience.

- The **script** is the heart of the *Readers' Theater* volume. This is the reproducible four- or five-page text that students will read during rehearsals and performances. You may wish to read the script aloud to students before assigning parts and beginning rehearsal readings. Once you have read through the script as a group, you may wish to assign students to work independently in small groups while you interact with other student groups.

- Two or three pages of follow-up **activities** may be assigned once students have completed a first reading of the script. Activities are designed to be completed independently, and may be conducted while you provide individualized or small-group instruction or hold a rehearsal with another group of students.

Meeting Individual Needs

Struggling readers may be partnered with one or more stronger readers who all read the same role together. This group support is often enough to allow struggling readers to participate fully in the activity. Struggling readers may also be able to independently read parts that have a repeating refrain or a simple rhyme pattern.

Students acquiring English may benefit from using the same approaches as for struggling readers. In addition, you may wish to create an audio recording of the script to provide English learners the opportunity to listen to fluent English pronunciation of the script as they follow along with the written text.

Accelerated learners may be challenged to transform *Readers' Theater* scripts into fully-staged productions by adding stage directions, planning props and sets, and even developing or expanding the existing dialog. You might also use such students as "directors," helping to manage small-group rehearsals for class *Readers' Theater* productions.

Evaluating Student Performance

Use the templates provided on pages 5 and 6 to help students plan and evaluate their performances. You may copy and distribute the templates just as they are, or use them to guide you in leading a class discussion about the criteria for evaluating *Readers' Theater* performances. Students may also develop their own iconography (e.g., one or two thumbs up, thumbs down, 1 to 5 stars, etc.) to rate their own performances and those of their classmates. Encourage students to be thoughtful in providing feedback, stressing the importance of sharing ways to improve, as well as highlighting successful aspects of the performance. You may wish to conduct performance reviews during the rehearsal stage in order to give students an opportunity to incorporate suggestions for improvement. You may also wish to compare those comments to feedback following the final performance. Use the template on page 7 to conduct your own assessment of students' acquisition of language arts skills during *Readers' Theater* activities.

NOTE: Reproduce this page so each student can check off the various steps in preparing a *Readers' Theater* performance. With emergent readers, be sure to read the checklist items aloud while students follow along and mark their pages.

Pre-performance Checklist

Name _____

1. Did you listen to a reading of the script?
   ☐ **Yes**
   ☐ **No** – Ask your teacher, another adult, or a classmate to read it to you.

2. Did you highlight all your lines in the script?
   ☐ **Yes**
   ☐ **No** – Use a highlighting pen to go over all your lines.

3. Did you mark places where you must pause between lines?
   ☐ **Yes**
   ☐ **No** – Use a mark like this: / /

4. Have you collected any materials or props that you will use?
   ☐ **Yes**
   ☐ **No** – Ask your teacher or other cast members for ideas if you need help.

5. Have you chosen and practiced any movements, faces, or speaking styles you will use?
   ☐ **Yes**
   ☐ **No** – Ask your teacher or other cast members for ideas if you need help.

6. Have you practiced reading your lines with expression?
   ☐ **Yes**
   ☐ **No** – Try out your ideas with a partner or another cast member.

7. Have you participated in a rehearsal and gotten performance feedback?
   ☐ **Yes**
   ☐ **No** – Have a reviewer focus on your participation in the play. After you get feedback, find ways to make changes to improve your performance.

Performance Review Template

Date: _____   Title of play: _____

☐ Rehearsal
☐ Performance

1. I am reviewing
   ☐ one reader   Name: _____   Role: _____
   ☐ the entire performance

2. I could see the reader(s).
   ☐ Yes
   ☐ Needs improvement   Name(s): _____

3. I could hear the reader(s).
   ☐ Yes
   ☐ Needs to speak more loudly   Name(s): _____

4. I could understand the reader(s).
   ☐ Yes
   ☐ Needs to speak more clearly   Name(s): _____

5. The reader(s) used good expression.
   ☐ Yes
   ☐ Needs to improve   Name(s): _____

6. The use of gestures was
   ☐ just right
   ☐ not enough; use more
   ☐ too much; use fewer   Name(s): _____

Other comments:

_____

_____

_____

_____

Assessing Oral Presentations

As you observe students during rehearsals or performances, focus on the following areas in assessing individual students.

Date: _____

Title of play: _____

☐ Rehearsal

☐ Performance

Name: _____ Role: _____

1. Student speaks clearly.	☐ Yes	☐ Needs improvement
2. Student speaks at appropriate pace.	☐ Yes	☐ Needs improvement
3. Student speaks fluently, using appropriate intonation, expression, and emphasis.	☐ Yes	☐ Needs improvement
4. Student enlivens reading with gestures and facial expressions.	☐ Yes	☐ Needs improvement
5. Student prepared and used appropriate props.	☐ Yes	☐ Not applicable
6. Student participated actively in rehearsals.	☐ Yes	☐ Needs improvement
7. Student contributed appropriately to this production.	☐ Yes	☐ Needs improvement

Other comments: _____

_____

_____

_____

Now Presenting...

Why Bear Has a Stumpy Tail

This is an old Norse folktale that explains how the bear got its short tail. Like so many other folktales, the story features a clever, tricky fox.

Setting the Stage

Background

Tell children that from earliest times, people all over the world have made up stories to explain how things came to be as they are. You might wish to point out Norway on a map and note its proximity to the frozen Arctic. Tell students that the cold weather in Norway is an important part of this tale.

Staging

Clear two areas for staging, one to represent the forest and another to represent the frozen lake.

Encore

After reading or performing this script, children may enjoy reading or hearing other *pour quoi* tales—stories that explain the origin of things. You might wish to work with individual students or a group to develop their own original stories in this genre.

Vocabulary

You may wish to introduce and discuss the following words before reading the script, or explain them during the first reading:

frozen: turned into ice or covered with ice

sit tight: to wait patiently

sting: a sharp or pricking feeling of pain

stream: a small river

stump: the part that is left after the rest has been cut off

tingle: to have a prickling or stinging feeling, especially from the cold

trundle: to walk with a rolling movement

Make sure children are familiar with these animals (use pictures if they are not):

bear

fish

fox

groundhog

rabbit

Now Presenting...

Why Bear Has a Stumpy Tail

Clever Fox tricks Bear into losing his long and beautiful tail.

Characters

Narrator 1 .... _____

Narrator 2 .... _____

Narrator 3 .... _____

Bear .... _____

Rabbit .... _____

Mouse......................... _____

Groundhog................... _____

Fox............................. _____

Why Bear Has a Stumpy Tail

Characters

Narrator 1	Rabbit
Narrator 2	Mouse
Narrator 3	Groundhog
Bear	Fox

Narrator 1: Long, long ago in the time before time, Bear had a beautiful tail.

Narrator 2: It was a long tail. It was a bushy tail.

Narrator 3: Bear was very proud of his tail.

Narrator 1: One winter day he walked through the woods, swishing his beautiful tail behind him.

Bear: What a lovely tail I have! I do believe it is the most beautiful tail in all the forest.

Rabbit: Yes, Bear, it is a lovely tail. It is nicer than my little cotton puff of a tail.

Mouse: It is nicer than my little rope of a tail.

Groundhog: You've got me beat, Bear. I barely have a tail at all.

Bear: Lucky me to have such a fancy tail!

Narrator 2: All this time, Fox was hiding behind a tree, listening.

Narrator 3: Fox knew that his own tail was really the most beautiful in the forest.

Narrator 1: It was a red, bushy tail with a lovely white tip.

Narrator 2: Fox was very clever. He decided to teach Bear a lesson.

Narrator 3: Fox slipped between the trees and down to the stream.

Narrator 1: The water in the stream was moving fast. It was not frozen over.

Narrator 2: Clever Fox quickly caught six fat fish.

Narrator 3: Fox trotted off into the forest to find Bear.

Narrator 1: He found Bear sitting alone on a large tree stump.

Fox: Hello, Bear.

Bear: Hello, Fox. Those fine fish will make a good supper. Where did you get them?

Fox: I caught them in the lake.

Bear: In the lake? The lake is frozen over. How can you catch fish in the lake?

Fox: It is easy. Just do as I tell you. Go down to the lake. Cut a hole in the ice. Sit down and drop your tail into the hole.

Bear: Brrr! That sounds cold!

Fox: Indeed it is. At first your tail will tingle. But you must sit tight.

Bear: How long must I stay there?

Fox: Oh, a long time. Your tail will sting and burn. But that is a good sign. It means the fish are biting.

Bear: I will do it! I want some fish for dinner.

Fox: Good. To be sure that you have enough fish, stay until sundown. Then jump up and pull your tail quickly out of the hole.

Bear: Thank you, Fox.

Narrator 2: Bear trundled off to the lake.

Narrator 3: He did everything Fox told him to do.

Narrator 2: He cut a hole in the ice. He dropped his tail in the hole.

Narrator 2: He sat on the ice and waited.

Bear: My tail is beginning to tingle, just as Fox said it would.

Narrator 3: Rabbit, Mouse, and Groundhog came out of the forest.

Rabbit: What are you doing, Bear?

Mouse: Why are you sitting on the ice?

Bear: I am fishing. I am going to have a fine feast for my dinner.

Groundhog: It's too cold for me! I'm going home.

Rabbit: Me, too! Good luck with your fishing.

Mouse: Good-bye, Bear!

Narrator 2: Bear waved good-bye to his friends. He sat on the ice and waited.

Bear: Ooh, now my tail is starting to sting. The fish must be biting!

Narrator 3: Bear closed his eyes and dreamed of a big platter filled with crispy, fried fish.

Narrator 1: After a while, Bear opened his eyes and looked at the sky.

Bear: The sun is going down. Now I can take my fish and go home.

Narrator 2: Bear tried to stand up, but his tail was stuck in the ice.

Bear: Fox said I would have to pull hard to bring up the fish.

Narrator 3: Bear gathered all his strength and jumped up suddenly.

Narrator 1: He tumbled over on the ice.

Narrator 2: Quickly, he looked around at his tail.

Narrator 3: He expected to see his beautiful tail covered with speckled fish.

Narrator 1: Instead he saw only a little stump! The rest of his magnificent tail remained frozen in the lake.

Narrator 2: And from that day to this, every bear has a short, stumpy tail.

Name _____

Animal Tails

Complete each animal by drawing its tail. Then write each animal's name.

fox	rabbit	mouse	bear

1. _____

2. _____

3. _____

4. _____

Animal Names

Write each animal's name in the correct boxes.

| fox | bear | fish |
| groundhog | mouse | rabbit |

Now Presenting...

Math at Farmers' Market

Two children, a shopping list, and a $20 bill add up to fun with math at a local farmers' market.

Setting the Stage

Background

Invite children to share about any experiences they have had with shopping at a farmers' market. You might also encourage them to tell about a time when they had money of their own that they could decide how to spend.

Staging

You may wish to have real or imitation produce on hand to help identify each of the sellers. The sellers may prepare cards with produce prices written on them for the audience to see. You might also like to work with the class to create posters of each of the math calculations that Tori and Tom perform during their shopping trip. The narrator could hold them up for the audience to see at that point in the script.

Encore

After reading this script, children may enjoy further exploration of the marketing topic by reading *Farmers' Market* by Paul Brett Johnson and *To Market, To Market* by Anne Miranda.

Vocabulary

Introduce and discuss the following words before reading the script:

ma'am: a polite name to use when speaking to a woman; short for "madam"

neighborhood: an area where people live in homes near each other

produce: fresh fruits and vegetables

sir: a polite name to use when speaking to a man

Now Presenting...

Math at Farmers' Market

When Mom gives Tori and Tom a shopping list and $20.00, will they be able to buy themselves a treat? Come along to Farmers' Market and find out!

Characters

Narrator .... _____

Tori (a first-grader)............. _____

Tom .... _____
(Tori's brother, a fourth-grader)

Mom................................... _____
(Tori and Tom's mother)

Lettuce Seller..................... _____

Tomato Seller .... _____

Berry Seller........................ _____

Flower Seller...................... _____

Math at Farmers' Market

······················· **Characters** ·······················

Narrator	Lettuce Seller
Tori	Tomato Seller
Tom	Berry Seller
Mom	Flower Seller

Narrator: Every Tuesday, farmers bring their fruits, flowers, and vegetables to the school parking lot. Families in the neighborhood come to buy their produce for the week. Today, Mom has asked Tori and Tom to shop while she sells eggs from the family's hen.

Mom: Tom, here is the shopping list. Tori, here is a $20.00 bill. Tom, see if you can help Tori practice counting the change. Please choose the produce carefully, and stay together. I'll meet you back here in 30 minutes. Have fun! In fact, buy yourselves a treat if you have enough money.

Tori and Tom: OK, Mom.

Tori: *(to Tom)* Wow! We're off. What's on the list?

Tom: *(reading from the list)* A head of lettuce, two onions, a box of tomatoes, three boxes of berries, and a bunch of sunflowers.

Tori: Let's start at the top. Do you see anyone with lettuce to sell?

Tom: There's some over there.

Tori: Excuse me, sir. How much is your lettuce?

Lettuce Seller: It's $1.00 for a small head and $2.00 for a large head.

Tom: Tori, what do you think? Shall we buy the small head or the large head?

Tori: Well, this lettuce is fresh. It looks good. We love salad. So let's get the big head. *(to the seller)* Sir, we'll take a large head.

Narrator: Tori hands the seller the $20.00 bill.

Lettuce Seller: Thank you. Here's your lettuce. And here's your change.

Tori: Thank you!

Tom: Tori, Mom said to count the change.

Tori: Well, he gave me a $10.00 bill, a $5.00 bill, and three $1.00 bills.

Tom: So here's how we count it: 10 plus 5 is 15. And 15 plus 3 is 18.

Tori: Then $18.00 plus the $2.00 we spent makes $20.00. So $18.00 in change is right.

Tom: Perfect! Onions and tomatoes are next on the list.

Tori: There are onions. And I see tomatoes, too. *(to the seller)* Ma'am, we'd like two onions and a box of tomatoes.

Tomato Seller: My onions go for 25¢ each, and the tomatoes are $1.50 per box.

Tori: Let's see . . . 25¢ plus 25¢ is 50¢. And 50¢ plus $1.50 is $2.00 even, right?

Tom: You've got it, Tori!

Tori: Choose the fullest basket with the brightest tomatoes, Tom. I'll pay.

Narrator: Tori hands the seller two $1.00 bills.

Tom: How much do we have left, Tori?

Tori: We still have the $10.00 bill, the $5.00 bill, and a $1.00 bill. That's 10 plus 5 . . . 15, plus one more is 16.

Tom: Good job! Now all we have to find are the berries and the sunflowers.

Tori: And a treat for us—If we have money left over.

Tom: Look over there. See that sign? *(reading the sign)* "All berries. One box for $2.50. Three boxes for $6.00."

Tori: Is that a good deal? We need three boxes.

Tom: Well, if we spend $6.00 for three boxes, that's $2.00 for each box. If we just bought one box, it would cost $2.50. So that IS a good deal. *(to the berry seller)* We'll take three boxes, please.

Berry Seller: I can see you two are a couple of smart shoppers! That'll be $6.00 even.

Tori: I'll give him the $5.00 bill and a $1.00 bill to make $6.00.

Tom: You're getting pretty good at this, Tori! *(to the berry seller)* Thanks a lot! *(to Tori)* OK, Tori. We had $16.00 and we just spent $6.00. How much do we have left?

Tori: That's easy: 16 minus 6 is 10. And here's our $10.00 bill.

Tom: And there are the sunflowers!

Tori: How much for a bunch of sunflowers, please?

Flower Seller: For you, just $4.00.

Tori: You can take it from this $10.00 bill, then.

Flower Seller: And here's your change, young lady. Have a great afternoon!

Tori: Thanks.

Tom: Well, we've gotten everything on the list. Mom expects us back in about 10 minutes. Do we have enough money for a treat?

Tori: Well, we have a $5.00 bill and a $1.00 bill. I know why—because 10 minus 4 is 6.

Tom: Right again! Hey—I know what we can buy! Look, there's the hand-cranked ice-cream booth. We can get a super cone for $2.00 each.

Tori: And 2 plus 2 is 4. That means we'll even have $2.00 left to give back to Mom.

Tom: You sure have gotten the hang of shopping at Farmers' Market. I bet Mom's going to ask us to shop every week!

Tori: As long as we get a treat, that's fine with me!

Name _____

Farmers' Market Math

Lettuce
$2.00/head

Onions
25¢ each

Sunflowers
$4/bunch

Tomatoes
$1.50/box

Berries
$2.00/box

Write the price of each item on the list. Add up the total.
Then circle the amount of money you will spend.

1 head
  of lettuce   _____

1 onion   _____

1 bunch of
  sunflowers   _____

Total $_____

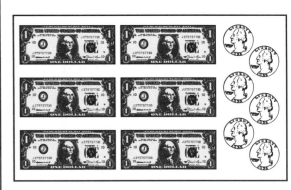

1 box of
  berries   _____

1 box of
  tomatoes   _____

Total $_____

1 bunch of
  sunflowers   _____

2 onions   _____

Total $_____

     Readers' Theater, Grade 1 • EMC 3306

Name _____

What Can You Buy?

Read the amount of money in each box. What could you buy for that amount? Draw a picture in each box.

$5.00	**50¢**
$2.50	**$10.00**

Now Presenting...

Stagecoach Mary

Mary Fields was born into slavery in Tennessee in 1832. As a woman, she grew to be six feet tall, moved to Montana, and had many larger-than-life adventures.

11 parts

Setting the Stage

Background

Tell children that this script is based on stories told about a woman who really lived in the United States over a hundred years ago. Mary Fields was born as a slave in Tennessee, but later moved to Montana as a free woman. Explain to students that in 1895, when Mary moved there, few people lived in Montana. Miners and homesteaders were trying hard to make a living in this remote and wild country. Mary provided an important service for these settlers: she delivered the mail, and her wagon was always on schedule, just like the stagecoach. Stagecoach Mary, as she came to be known, became a legend in her own time.

Vocabulary

You may wish to introduce and discuss the following words before reading the script, or explain them during the first reading:

convent: a building where nuns live together

deed: a document that says who legally owns a piece of property

homesteader: a person who settles on land that is being developed for the first time

miner: a person whose work is to dig gold, coal, or other minerals from the earth

nun: a woman who lives and works as part of a religious organization and who has dedicated her life to serving God

plains: flat, open grasslands

prairie: another name for *plains*

stagecoach: a coach pulled by horses over a regular route and on a set schedule

Now Presenting...

Stagecoach Mary

A large woman has some larger-than-life adventures.

Characters

Narrator 1.......................... _____

Narrator 2.......................... _____

Narrator 3.......................... _____

Mary................................. _____

Nun 1 .... _____

Nun 2 .... _____

Postmaster........................ _____

Miner................................ _____

Homesteader Sam............. _____

Matilda .... _____

Cowboy............................. _____

Stagecoach Mary

.... **Characters** ....

Narrator 1	Postmaster
Narrator 2	Miner
Narrator 3	Homesteader Sam
Mary	Matilda
Nun 1	Cowboy
Nun 2	

Narrator 1: The year is 1895. The place is Cascade, Montana.

Narrator 2: Our story is about Mary Fields. She was born a slave in Tennessee.

Mary: That was a long time ago. Now I do as I please. I work for the nuns at the convent. I chop wood. I build fences. I'm six feet tall and as strong as any man. I can do anything, and I'm afraid of nothing!

Nun 1: Mary, I have a job for you.

Mary: Sure thing. What can I do for you?

Nun 2: We need some supplies.

Nun 1: Can you take the wagon to Great Falls to get the things we need?

Mary: I can do it with one hand tied behind my back!

Nun 2: Here's the list. We need beans, cornmeal, and molasses.

Mary: I'll hitch up Mose, my good old mule, and we'll take off this evening. I like to travel when it's cool.

Narrator 3: As soon as the sun went down, Mary set out across the prairie.

Narrator 1: She went to Great Falls, bought the supplies, and rested until nightfall.

Narrator 2: Then she started home.

Narrator 3: Around midnight, Mary heard the howling of wolves.

Narrator 1: The sound grew closer and closer.

Narrator 2: Mose got very nervous.

Narrator 3: When the wolves came into view, Mose took off running.

Narrator 1: The wagon tipped over. Mary fell out. So did the beans, the cornmeal, and the molasses.

Mary: Doggone it, Mose! You don't need to be afraid of a few measly wolves. Now calm down!

Narrator 2: While the wolves circled the wrecked wagon, Mary built a campfire.

Narrator 3: Now and then, she fired a shot from her trusty rifle into the inky darkness.

Mary: *(laughing)* Go on, you old wolves! You'll get out of here if you know what's good for you.

Narrator 1: As soon as the sun came up, Mary fixed up the wagon, hitched up Mose, and went on her way.

Nun 1: Here comes Mary!

Nun 2: The wagon looks a mite ragged. Did you have any trouble?

Mary: None I couldn't handle!

Narrator 2: The nuns shivered as Mary told the story of the wolves.

Narrator 3: But Mary just laughed.

Narrator 1: It so happened that the postmaster was visiting the nuns.

Narrator 2: He was looking for a man to deliver mail.

Narrator 3: When he saw Mary and heard her tale, he knew he did not need to look any longer.

Postmaster: Mary, would you like to go to work for me?

Mary: Doing what?

Postmaster: Delivering the mail! The miners and cowboys and homesteaders like to get letters from home. Will you drive the mail?

Mary: Well, I like my job helping the nuns. But delivering the mail sounds pretty good, too. Yes, I believe I will try!

Postmaster: Great! Here is a packet of letters and a map. Go ahead and get started.

Narrator 1: Mary hitched up old Mose and off she went.

Narrator 2: First, she went to a gold mining town.

Miner: Look here, boys. We've got mail! Yippee!

Narrator 3: Next, she traveled to a homestead cabin.

Homesteader Sam: Glory be, Matilda! Come quick! There's a letter from your sister and one from Aunt Jo!

Matilda: *(to Mary)* Oh, thank you, ma'am. Thank you so much.

Mary: My pleasure. See you next week.

Narrator 1: Next, Mary and Mose trotted out on the plains, where some cowboys were camped with their herd.

Cowboy: I must be seeing things! How did you find us way out here?

Mary: The mail must go through. Look for me again soon!

Narrator 2: Well, it wasn't long before everyone knew they could depend on Mary.

Narrator 3: She made her rounds, regular as could be.

Narrator 1: Pretty soon, folks started to call her Stagecoach Mary, because she always ran right on schedule, just like the stagecoach.

Narrator 2: It didn't matter if the wind blew, the snow flew, or the creeks rose.

Narrator 3: Stagecoach Mary and Mose found their way to all the folks along their route.

Narrator 1: She carried land deeds and mining claims. Why, some say she helped open that country up!

Mary: Indeed I did, with a little help from good old Mose!

Community Helper

Draw a picture that shows how Mary helped her community.
Write a sentence telling about your picture.

_____

_____

Name _____

Mary and Mose

Mary and **Mose** both start with the letter **m**. Can you find all these words that also start with **m**?

mail	map
Mary	miner
money	moon
Mose	mouse

o	m	a	i	l	u	e
m	o	s	e	y	m	m
i	m	o	o	n	o	o
n	u	m	k	o	n	u
o	h	i	n	w	e	s
m	a	n	u	q	y	e
a	s	e	y	i	r	d
p	h	r	m	a	r	y

Now Presenting...

All Through the Year

When her magic mirror cannot give her the answer, a queen sets her advisors the task of determining which is the best season of the year.

Setting the Stage

Background

Guide students in a discussion of the four seasons. Discuss the characteristics of each season and which months fall in each season. Encourage students to identify the season in which their birthday falls.

Staging

Designate two areas on the stage, one for the queen's room and another for the chamber in which the queen's advisors deliberate.

Vocabulary

You may wish to introduce and discuss the following words before reading the script, or explain them during the first reading:

chamber: a special room for meetings

crocus: a flower that blooms in the spring

jester: a person who entertains kings and queens with jokes and silly behavior

wise: someone who has good judgment and lots of knowledge

Now Presenting...

All Through the Year

Which is the best season of the year? A queen tries to learn the answer to this question.

Characters

Narrator .... _____

Queen Anna .... _____

Mirror .... _____

Jester................................ _____

Archie (a Wise Man) .... _____

Reggie (a Wise Man)......... _____

Carolina (a Wise Woman) .. _____

Sofia (a Wise Woman)........ _____

All Through the Year

.... **Characters** ....

Narrator

Queen Anna

Mirror

Jester

Archie

Reggie

Carolina

Sofia

Narrator: Queen Anna looked out the window at the falling snow.

Queen Anna: My kingdom looks beautiful in winter.
I think winter must be the most beautiful season of all.

Jester: It is quite beautiful, Your Highness.

Queen Anna: I know! I shall ask my magic mirror.
Mirror, Mirror on the wall.
Which is the very best season of all?

Mirror: All through the year the seasons change.
Each brings its own delight.
I cannot tell you which is best.
No answer would be right.

Narrator: Queen Anna was very surprised.

Queen Anna: What do you mean, there's no right answer?
You are supposed to know everything, Mirror!

Narrator: But the mirror was silent.

Queen Anna: Very well. Jester, call in the Wise Men and Women of the kingdom. They will know the answer!

Narrator: The Wise Men and Women came running.

Wise Men and Women: At your service, Your Highness. What may we do for you?

Queen Anna: I have a simple question for you to answer.

Wise Men and Women: Gladly, Your Highness.

Queen Anna: Which is the very best season of the year? Is it winter? Is it spring? Is it summer? Or is it fall?

Archie: That is a difficult question to answer, Your Highness.

Carolina: Indeed, it is.

Reggie: It's almost impossible!

Sofia: We must go to our chamber to discuss this question. We will return in one hour.

Narrator: The Wise Men and Women hurried off to their chamber.

Archie: Let us take each season, one by one.

Carolina: All right. What is spring?

Sofia: Spring is dancing in a rain shower...

Reggie: ...and splashing in a mud puddle.

Carolina: Spring is a field of daffodils...

Archie: ...or the first crocus peeking through the snow.

Reggie: Spring is a time when the world turns new.

Carolina: *(sigh)* Surely spring is the best season.

Archie: Perhaps! But we must be certain. What about summer?

Archie: Summer is fireflies in the evening…

Sofia: …and running through the sprinklers. I **love** to run through the sprinklers!

Reggie: Summer is green grass and picnics and popsicles...

Carolina: *(softly)* Summer is pretty great.

Archie: Let's go on. We must talk about fall.

Sofia: Fall is a shower of golden leaves.

Carolina: Fall is a fat, round, bright orange pumpkin.

Reggie: Fall is soup for lunch...

 Readers' Theater, Grade 1 • EMC 3306

Archie: ...and apples that crunch!

Sofia: Fall is playing football and raking leaves.

Reggie: Fall is fantastic!

Carolina: But we can't forget winter.

Archie: Ahh, winter.

Sofia: Winter is catching snowflakes on your tongue.

Reggie: Winter is building a snowman...

Carolina: ...or cuddling up with a good book.

Archie: Winter is hot chocolate...with a marshmallow!

Sofia: Winter is sledding and skating and frosty air.

Archie: Winter is wonderful.

Reggie: ALL of the seasons are magnificent. There is no right answer to this question!

Carolina: Let's go tell the queen.

Sofia: She won't be happy.

Narrator: The Wise Men and Women went back to see the queen.

Archie: *(bowing)* Your Highness, we are sorry. There is no right answer to the question.

Queen Anna: What do you mean, there's no right answer? You are supposed to know everything!

Jester: Your Highness, I think I know the answer.

Queen Anna: *(laughing)* All right, Jester. What is your answer?

Jester: The seasons change all through the year. The one that's best is the one that's here!

Carolina: The jester is right! No wonder we couldn't decide!

Reggie: Each season is best in its turn.

Queen Anna: So for the moment, winter is best! Let's all go out and build a snow castle!

Narrator: And that is what they did.

Name _____

The Four Seasons

Draw a picture to show something special about each season of the year. Label each picture with the name of the season.

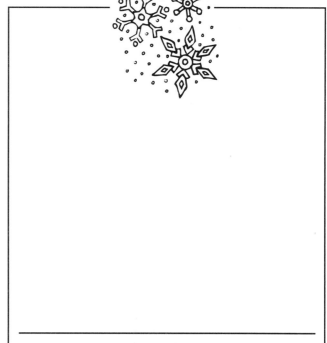

42

Name _____

Seasonal Sums

Solve each problem. Hint: Draw a picture if you need help.

1. In the spring, Archie planted a garden. He planted 2 packets of carrot seeds, 3 packets of lettuce seeds, and 1 packet of tomato seeds. How many packets of seeds did he plant?

_____ + _____ + _____ = _____

2. In the summer, Carolina had a picnic with her friends. She made 2 sandwiches for Reggie, 2 sandwiches for Sofia, 1 sandwich for Archie, and 1 sandwich for herself. How many sandwiches did she make?

___ + ___ + ___ + ___ = _____

3. In the fall, Reggie went to the pumpkin patch. He bought 3 pumpkins for the jester and 3 pumpkins for Carolina. Archie and Sofia did not want any pumpkins. How many pumpkins did Reggie buy?

___ + ___ + ___ = _____

4. In the winter, Queen Anna baked some pies. She baked 1 pie for each of the 4 wise people. She baked 2 pies for the jester. How many pies did she bake?

___ + ___ + ___ + ___ + ___ = ___

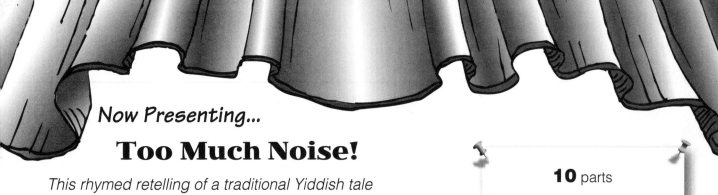

Now Presenting...

Too Much Noise!

This rhymed retelling of a traditional Yiddish tale teaches that sometimes things have to get worse before you realize that they weren't all that bad to begin with!

Setting the Stage

Background

Tell children that this story has been told for hundreds of years in many different ways. It was traditionally told by the Jews of Eastern Europe, who spoke a language called *Yiddish*. The script includes words in Yiddish that may be familiar to children with European Jewish heritage: *zayde* (ZAY-duh, "grandpa"), *bubbe* (BUH-bee, "grandma"), *rebbe* (REH-bee, "teacher," also used for Jewish spiritual leaders), and *oy* (an expression of exasperation).

Explain that this story teaches a lesson about learning to face problems and difficult situations. After presenting the script, lead a discussion with children about the lesson this story teaches. Help the group state the story's lesson with a simple sentence such as, "When you think things are bad, remember—they could always be worse!"

Staging

Set the family's and Rebbe's homes at opposite ends of the staging area. The "animals" may move into or out of the house, as the script indicates. You might provide the mother with a broom and have the grandparents sit in rocking chairs or hold canes (for "rocking and tapping"). An additional sound effects crew may help add to the cacophony by chiming in on the rhyming refrain of sound words.

Encore

After reading or performing this rhyming version of the traditional tale, children may enjoy hearing or reading other versions, such as *Too Much Noise* by Ann McGovern or *It's Too Noisy!* by Joanna Cole.

Vocabulary

You may wish to introduce and discuss the following words before reading the script, or explain them during the first reading:

bawl: to cry loudly

implore: to beg

patience: being able to wait without complaining

poke: to push or jab with a finger

pout: to sulk or show that you are unhappy

rock: to move back and forth in a rocking chair; to move a baby's cradle back and forth

Now Presenting...

Too Much Noise!

How much is too much? That depends on how you look at it. The man in this tale learns that "too much" may be just right, after all!

Characters

Storyteller .... _____

Mother .... _____

Grandparents .... _____

_____

Children .... _____

_____

Father .... _____

Rebbe .... _____

Animals .... _____

_____

Too Much Noise!

·························· **Characters** ··························

Storyteller   Father
Mother   Rebbe
Grandparents   Animals
Children

Storyteller: There once was a house so cozy and small.
And packed in the house, packed wall to wall,...

Mother: ...were a man and his wife, a boy and a girl,
a cute smiling babe with one soft, brown curl,...

Grandparents: ...Zayda and Bubbe, a dog and a cat,
two noisy crickets, and a long-tailed rat.

Storyteller: The house was not quiet.
In fact, you might say
the house was quite noisy
in a loud sort of way.
There was…

Children: ...shouting and joking, pouting and poking,

Mother: calling and sweeping, bawling and sleeping,

Grandparents: clapping and rocking, tapping and knocking.

All: There was too much noise!

Storyteller: Hands over his ears, the man ran outside.

Father: *(hands over ears)* Oy! I must have quiet!

Storyteller: The poor man cried.

Father: I'll ask the rebbe. He'll understand.
He'll know what to do. He'll give me a plan.

Storyteller: So that's just what he did.
He knocked on the door
and when it opened,
I heard him implore…

Father: …Rebbe, wise Rebbe, what can I do?
My house is too loud. My family? It grew!

Rebbe: It's easy to see. I know what you need.
Bring the chickens inside. Too noisy? Indeed!

Storyteller: The man blinked his eyes,
then he scratched his head,
but he went home and did
what the rebbe had said.
He gathered the hens
and the rooster, too.
He took them inside.

Mother: What a strange thing to do!
Now there was…

Children: ...shouting and joking, pouting and poking,

Mother: calling and sweeping, bawling and sleeping,

Grandparents: clapping and rocking, tapping and knocking,

Animals: clucking and hatching, crowing and scratching.

All: There was too much noise!

Father: *(hands over ears)* Oy! What shall I do?

Storyteller: He went back to the rebbe
to ask him once more.

Father: He's just got to help.

Storyteller: The man knocked on the door.

Father: Rebbe, wise Rebbe, what can be done?
The noise in my home just isn't fun!

Rebbe: There's no need to worry.
Now, don't get upset.
I have an answer.
You'll fix it yet.
The cow and the donkey,
and also the horse
should be inside your house.
You agree, of course!

Storyteller: The man blinked his eyes,
then he scratched his head,
but he went home and did
what the rebbe had said.
He herded the horse, the donkey, and cow.
He got them inside. He did it somehow.

Grandparents: What a strange thing to do!
Now there was…

Children: …shouting and joking, pouting and poking,

Mother: calling and sweeping, bawling and sleeping,

Grandparents: clapping and rocking, tapping and knocking,

Animals: clucking and hatching, crowing and scratching,
neighing and mooing, braying and mewing.

All: There was too much noise!

Father: *(hand over ears)* Oy! What can I do?

Storyteller: Once more to the rebbe the poor man did go.

Father: I must have some quiet. The rebbe must know.
Rebbe, wise Rebbe, what can I do?
I'm losing my mind and my patience, too.

Rebbe: Good man, don't give up. You must do as I say.
Put all of the animals outside today.

Storyteller: The man blinked his eyes,
then he scratched his head.
But once more he did
what the rebbe had said.
The chickens and rooster went out,
and the donkey did, too.
Then the horse and the cow,
and then he was through!
Now, there was just...

Children: ...shouting and joking, pouting and poking,

Mother: calling and sweeping, bawling and sleeping,

Grandparents: clapping and rocking, tapping and knocking.

Father: So peaceful, so quiet! So cozy, so nice!
Now our little house is a paradise!

Name _____

Animal Match

Match the name of the animal from the story with its picture.

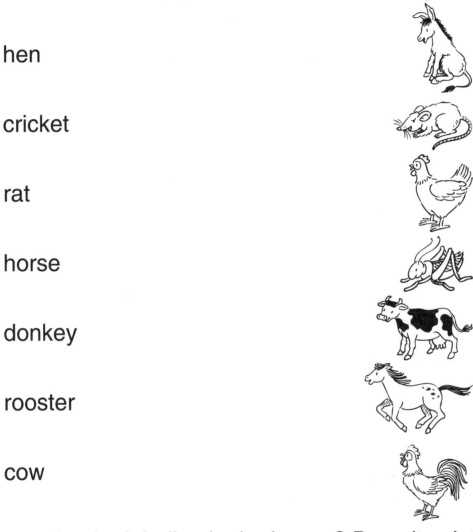

hen

cricket

rat

horse

donkey

rooster

cow

What other animal might live in the house? Draw its picture here.

Rhyming Noises

Here's a rhyme with words from the play. Copy a rhyming word from the box to fill in each blank.

bawling	braying	hatching
knocking	poking	

In that noisy little house there was

shouting and joking,

pouting and _____,

calling and sweeping,

_____ and sleeping,

clapping and rocking,

tapping and _____,

clucking and _____,

crowing and scratching,

neighing and mooing,

_____ and mewing.

There was too much noise!

Now Presenting...

The
Shark King's Son

Like many traditional tales from Hawai`i, this one features the Shark King, a character with many magical powers. For generations, this tale has been used to explain the origin of a blowhole near Waipio on the Big Island.

12 parts

Program .... page 54

Script .... pages 55–59

Activities .... pages 60 & 61

Setting the Stage

Background

Guide children in a discussion of folktales and fairy tales. Make sure they understand that they are stories that have been told for generations, and that the characters often include imaginary or magical beings with special powers. Encourage children to mention characters of this sort, such as the fairy godmother or witch in "Sleeping Beauty." Tell students that one of the characters in this play is a shark who can transform himself into a handsome man.

Point out Hawai`i on a map or globe, and tell children that "The Shark King's Son" is a story from Hawai`i. Help children note that Hawai`i is actually a collection of islands surrounded by the Pacific Ocean. If possible, show students some pictures of Hawai`i so they can better visualize the setting for this story.

Staging

Use a towel to make a simple cape for Nanave. Attach some bright-colored feathers to the towel, if available.

Vocabulary

Introduce and discuss the following words before reading the script:

blowhole: an opening in an undersea cave that leads to the surface; water sprays as it comes through a blowhole

cape: a piece of cloth that is fastened at the neck and drapes over the shoulders

chief: the leader of a tribe or group

feast: a fancy meal prepared for a special occasion where guests are invited

luau: a Hawaiian feast; it usually includes entertainment

magic: the use of spells and charms to try to control events

pool: a small pond

shark: a large ocean-dwelling fish with a tall dorsal fin; most sharks eat fish

superb: excellent

village: a group of houses out in the country or jungle

The Shark King's Son

The native people of Hawai`i have used this folktale to explain how a blowhole on the Big Island came to be.

Characters

Narrator 1 .... _____

Narrator 2 .... _____

Narrator 3 .... _____

The Shark King .... _____

Kalini .... _____

Nanave.............................. _____

Fisherman 1 .... _____

Fisherman 2 .... _____

Villagers .... _____

_____

_____

Village Chief...................... _____

The Shark King's Son

········· **Characters** ·········

Narrator 1	Nanave
Narrator 2	Fisherman 1
Narrator 3	Fisherman 2
The Shark King	Villagers
Kalini	Village Chief

Narrator 1: Long ago in a small Hawaiian village there lived a beautiful young woman named Kalini.

Narrator 2: One morning, the Shark King happened to see Kalini enjoying her morning swim in the ocean.

Narrator 3: The Shark King thought that Kalini was a very good swimmer for a human being.

Narrator 1: The Shark King had magical powers. He used them to turn himself into a tall, strong man.

Narrator 2: He threw a cape of bright feathers over his shoulders and followed Kalini to her village.

Narrator 3: The village chief welcomed the handsome stranger. A wonderful luau was planned in his honor.

Narrator 1: After the feasting, there were many games.

Narrator 2: The Shark King won every contest.

Narrator 3: Later that night, the Shark King went to Kalini.

Shark King: Kalini, you are the best swimmer and loveliest person I have ever seen. Will you marry me?

Narrator 1: Kalini agreed. She and the Shark King built a home near a deep pool in the forest.

Narrator 2: Each day, Kalini and the Shark King would swim in the pool. They were very happy.

Narrator 3: Sometimes the Shark King would dive deep underwater. He would stay underwater for a very long time.

Narrator 1: This frightened Kalini, for she feared he would drown.

Kalini: Husband, why do you stay underwater for so long? It worries me.

Shark King: Kalini, I am a superb swimmer. I will not drown. Someday we will have a son. I am making a special place for him at the bottom of the pool.

Narrator 2: Time passed. One day Kalini told her husband that she would soon give birth to a baby.

Shark King: *(sadly)* I must go away now. Someday you will understand. Raise our son well. And make sure that he always wears my feathered cape.

Narrator 3: Kalini did not understand, but she agreed to her husband's request.

Narrator 1: When the baby was born, Kalini named him Nanave. She noticed that he had a strange mark on his back. It looked exactly like a shark's mouth.

Kalini: Now I understand! My husband was the Shark King. No wonder he wanted his son to wear the cape!

Narrator 2: Kalini kept her word. Nanave never went anywhere without the cape.

Narrator 3: Each morning Nanave followed the fishermen to the shore.

Nanave: Good morning, Fishermen. Where are you going fishing today?

Fisherman 1: We are going out by the reef to the north of the island.

Fisherman 2: There are many fish there. We should have a good catch.

Narrator 1: Nanave waved until the fishermen were out of sight.

Narrator 2: Then he ran up the forest path and jumped into the pool by his house. He stayed in the pool for many hours.

Narrator 3: As time passed, the fishermen were able to catch fewer and fewer fish.

Villagers: We are hungry! Why aren't you catching enough fish for us to eat?

Fisherman 2: Something is wrong! I think there is some bad magic in the village.

Chief: I know what to do.

Narrator 1: The chief spread a carpet of leaves on the ground. He told all the people in the village to walk on the leaves.

Narrator 2: The chief knew that human feet would make marks on the soft leaves. The feet of a magical being would make no marks.

Narrator 3: Nanave was afraid to take the test. When it was his turn, he ran quickly across the carpet of leaves.

Narrator 1: He ran so fast that he slipped. A man who was standing nearby tried to catch Nanave as he fell.

Narrator 2: The cape slipped off Nanave's shoulders. Everyone could see the shark's mouth on his back.

Chief: Seize him!

Fisherman 1: Here is the one who has been chasing away our fish!

Villagers: Don't let him get away!

Narrator 3: Nanave ran fast. He dove into the forest pool.

Narrator 1: The villagers threw rocks into the pool until it was full.

Villagers: That is the end of him!

Chief: Nanave can never trouble us again!

Narrator 2: But Kalini knew that her son was not dead. She remembered that his father had made a special place for him at the bottom of the pool.

Narrator 3: She knew that the special place was a tunnel that led to the ocean.

Narrator 1: She knew that Nanave had gone to find his father, the Shark King.

Name _____

Picture Dictionary

Draw a picture to show the meaning of each word.

feast	**pool**
village	**chief**

Name _____

How Did They Feel?

Use the words in the box to complete the sentences.

sad	surprised	happy	afraid	worried	angry

1. When Kalini and the Shark King swam in the pool, they

felt _____.

2. When the Shark King stayed underwater for a long time,

Kalini felt _____.

3. When the Shark King told Kalini that he must go away, he

felt _____.

4. When the cape slipped off Nanave's shoulders, everyone

was _____.

5. When the fishermen learned that Nanave had chased

away the fish, they felt _____.

6. When the villagers ran after Nanave, he felt _____.

Now Presenting...

Out in the Woods

Six friends use their five senses and their imaginations as they plan a camp-out in the woods.

Setting the Stage

Background

Guide students in a discussion of the five senses. Ask them to describe things they can see, hear, touch, taste, and smell at school. Then have them imagine things they might see, hear, touch, taste, and smell during a camp-out in the woods.

Staging

Use a paper plate to create a simple bear mask for the bear to wear. (Note: The bear does not have a speaking role.) Model reading the script in a rhythmic, chanting style and reading Marvin's part with lots of feeling, getting louder with each repetition. Direct other actors to ignore Marvin until the very end.

Vocabulary

You may wish to introduce and discuss the following words before reading the script, or explain them during the first reading:

burble: to make a gurgling or bubbling sound

pebble: a small rock or stone

shaggy: covered with long fur or hair

woods: a forest

Out in the Woods

Join six good friends in their backyard as they plan an exciting adventure in the woods.

Characters

Sally.................................... _____

Ben .... _____

Marvin................................. _____

Tina.................................... _____

Rae Lynne .... _____

Sammy .... _____

Chorus .... _____

_____

_____

_____

Bear .... _____

Out in the Woods

································· **Characters** ·······················

Sally	Rae Lynne
Ben	Sammy
Marvin	Chorus
Tina	Bear

Sally: Let's go camping.

Chorus: Out in the woods. The big woods. The deep woods. The wonderful woods.

Ben: Let's go camping.

Chorus: Out in the woods.

Tina: What will we see there?

Chorus: Out in the woods. The big woods. The deep woods. The wonderful woods.

Marvin: *(softly)* We might see a bear there.

Chorus: Out in the woods.

Sammy: A big bear. A shaggy bear.

Marvin: *(a little louder)* We might see a bear there.

Chorus: Out in the woods.

Tina: What will we hear there?

Chorus: Out in the woods.

Rae Lynne: We might hear a hoot-owl.

Ben: Hooo! Hooo!

Sammy: We might hear a running stream.

Sally: Burble, burble, burble.

Rae Lynne: We might hear the wind blow.

Sammy: Whoosh, whoosh.

Marvin: *(a little louder)* And we might see a bear there!

Chorus: Out in the woods.

Tina: What will we smell there?

Chorus: Out in the woods.

Ben: We might smell a campfire.

Sally: Smoky, choky.

Sammy: We might smell a pine tree.

Rae Lynne: Nice and spicy.

Sally: We might smell the fresh air.

Ben: Clean and clear.

Chorus: Out in the woods. The big woods. The deep woods. The wonderful woods.

Marvin: *(louder still)* And we might see a bear there!

Chorus: Out in the woods.

Tina: What will we touch there?

Chorus: Out in the woods.

Rae Lynne: We might touch a pinecone.

Sammy: Prickly and scratchy.

Ben: We might touch the pebbles in the burbling stream.

Sally: Cool and round and hard and smooth.

Sammy: We might touch a feather that we find on the ground.

Rae Lynne: Soft and tickly.

Chorus: Out in the woods. The big woods. The deep woods. The wonderful woods.

Marvin: *(very loud)* And we might see a bear there!

Chorus: Out in the woods.

Tina: What will we taste there?

Chorus: Out in the woods.

Ben: We might taste a marshmallow.

Rae Lynne: Sticky and burnt.

Sammy: We might taste a hot dog.

Sally: Mustard and ketchup.

Rae Lynne: We might taste trail mix.

Sammy: Crunchy and chewy.

Chorus: Out in the woods. The big woods. The deep woods. The wonderful woods.

Marvin: *(almost yelling)* And we might see a bear there!

Chorus: Out in the woods.

Ben: *(pretending to set up tent)* We'll set up our tent.

Chorus: Out in the woods.

Sally: *(pretending to cook)* We'll cook our dinner.

Chorus: Out in the woods.

Rae Lynne: *(sitting down and holding hands over an imaginary fire)* We'll sit by the campfire.

Chorus: Out in the woods.

Marvin: *(really yelling)* But what are we going to do if we see a bear there?

(Bear enters from off stage. Everyone stops and looks at Marvin, then at the bear, and then at each other.)

Sammy: *(to the bear)* We'll say, "Hello, bear. Sit over there."

(The bear sits down obediently.)

Chorus: And we'll all be happy, out in the woods!

Name _____

Through the Woods

Help the children find the way through the woods to their campsite.

Find the bear. Write a sentence to tell where the bear is hiding.

_____

_____

Senses Match

Match each sense to the correct body part.

hear

touch

see

taste

smell

Write the best word to complete each sentence.

I hear with my _____.

I see with my _____.

I smell with my _____.

I taste with my _____.

I touch with my _____.

nose

mouth

hand

eyes

ears

Now Presenting...

Big Mose

This tall tale tells some of the heroics of a New York City firefighter who was so brave that he became legendary.

Setting the Stage

Background

Explain to children that Mose Humphrey—known as "Big Mose"—was a New York City firefighter who lived about 150 years ago. He was very brave and strong, and was known for his many amazing and heroic feats. Stories about Big Mose have gotten so exaggerated that they have turned into tall tales. Like most tall tales, there is usually some bit of truth in such stories.

Make sure children understand that during the 1800s, when this story takes place, horse-drawn wagons were the only fire trucks available in New York City. Explain that the Bowery is a New York City neighborhood.

Staging

Designate an area for the river and one for the fire. If possible, provide a bell for the streetcar conductor.

Encore

Children may enjoy hearing or reading other tall tales in collections such as *American Tall Tales* by Mary Pope Osborne (which includes a tale about Big Mose) or *Cut From the Same Cloth: American Women of Myth, Legend and Tall Tale* by Robert D. San Souci.

Vocabulary

You may wish to introduce and discuss the following words before reading the script, or explain them during the first reading:

clang: the loud, sharp ringing sound of a bell

current: a strong flow of water

dock: a large pier or wharf where ships arrive

gush: to flow out suddenly and in a large quantity

harness: the leather straps and metal pieces used to fasten a horse or mule to a wagon

hero: a person who is admired for his or her courage

sizzle: to make a hissing sound, especially when water comes in contact with something hot

stroke: a movement of the arms through the water while swimming

Now Presenting...

Big Mose

Even though New York City firefighter Mose Humphrey lived over 150 years ago, tales of his bravery are still told!

Characters

Narrator 1 .... _____

Narrator 2 .... _____

Mose .... _____

Jake .... _____

Woman.............................. _____

Rupert .... _____

Crowd............................... _____

_____

_____

Girl .... _____

Streetcar Conductor........... _____

People on the Streetcar ..... _____

_____

Big Mose

•••••••••••••••• Characters ••••••••••••••••

Narrator 1	Rupert
Narrator 2	Crowd
Mose	Girl
Jake	Streetcar Conductor
Woman	People on the Streetcar

Narrator 1: Big Mose was a firefighter. He lived in New York City more than 150 years ago.

Narrator 2: One day, Mose was polishing the fire wagon when Jake came rushing into the firehouse...

Jake: Mose, hitch up that wagon! Someone is yelling for help!

Narrator 1: Quickly, the firefighters slipped the big gray fire horses into their harnesses.

Narrator 2: They climbed onto the wagon and dashed toward the river. As they came closer, they heard a woman screaming.

Woman: Help, help! My little boy has fallen into the river!

Mose: Don't worry, ma'am. We'll save your little boy!

Jake: *(to Mose)* I don't know, Mose. Look, the current has carried him far down the stream. I don't know if you can get to him.

Narrator 1: Mose didn't answer. He just jumped right into the water.

Narrator 2: Mose began to swim. One stroke, two strokes, three strokes.

Narrator 1: In three swift strokes, Mose had reached the drowning child.

Narrator 2: He scooped him up in his powerful arms.

Woman: Thank you, Mose! You did it! You are my hero.

Crowd: Hooray for Mose, the firefighter hero!

Mose: *(shrugging his shoulders)* It's all in a day's work.

Narrator 1: The firefighters went back to the firehouse to rest. But they didn't get to rest for long.

Girl: *(out of breath)* Hurry, please hurry! There's a big fire up in the Bowery.

Rupert: Let's go, boys!

Narrator 2: Again, the big gray horses clattered through the streets.

Mose: This looks like a big fire.

Rupert: There sure is a lot of smoke.

Jake: I'll start pumping water from the wagon.

Rupert: We don't have enough water to put this one out. There's nothing we can do.

Mose: Oh yes, there is! Do what you can with the water we have. I'll be right back with more.

Jake: Where is he going?

Rupert: Who knows? Let's get busy!

Narrator 1: Jake and Rupert pumped water from the wagon into the flames.

Narrator 2: Mose ran straight toward the river. The smoke was thick and dark.

Narrator 1: As Mose ran he heard a bell clanging loudly.

Streetcar Conductor: *(ringing bell)* We need help! We're trapped!

People on the Streetcar: Help us! Help us!

Narrator 2: Mose ran toward the sound.

Narrator 1: He saw the streetcar through clouds of smoke and ash. The streetcar was surrounded by fire.

Mose: Hang on, everyone. I'll save you!

Narrator 2: Mose knelt down next to the streetcar.

Narrator 1: He slid the streetcar onto his shoulder.

Mose: Here we go. Now hold on!

Narrator 2: Slowly, Mose rose to his feet.

Narrator 1: On he went toward the river, the streetcar bouncing on his back.

Narrator 2: When he neared the river, he set the streetcar down.

Mose: Okay folks, you'll be safe here. I've got more work to do.

People on the Streetcar: Hooray for Big Mose, the firefighter hero!

Narrator 1: But Mose was already out of sight.

Narrator 2: He hurried on 'til he reached the riverbank. He grabbed a shovel from a tool shed near the docks.

Narrator 1: Big Mose began to dig.

Narrator 2: The dirt flew. The hole grew deeper. Soon Mose disappeared from sight.

Narrator 1: Big Mose dug and dug, faster and faster.

Narrator 2: Back at the fire, Jake and Rupert heard a strange noise. They felt the earth shift under their feet.

Narrator 1: Suddenly, Big Mose popped out of the ground with a shovel in his hand.

Mose: Clear the way, boys! I've brought you some water!

Narrator 2: With a rumble and a roar, the water of the Hudson River gushed out of the hole.

Narrator 1: The fire died to a sizzle.

Jake, Rupert, and Crowd: Hooray for Mose, the firefighter hero!

Mose: *(shrugging his shoulders)* It's all in a day's work.

Sound Off

Some words are just fun to say! These are words that imitate sounds. Read each word aloud. Draw a picture of something that you think makes that sound.

clang	**sizzle**
rumble	**clatter**

Big Mose, Firefighter Hero

The people that Mose helped called him a hero. Who is someone that you think of as a hero? Draw a picture and write a sentence that tells about your hero.

Now Presenting...

The Three Billy Goats Gruff

This traditional tale about three goats that vanquish a troll is enhanced by sound effects performed by a chorus.

Setting the Stage

Background

Invite children who are familiar with this traditional tale to outline the story's plot and action. Then tell children that the version they will be hearing includes sound effects words, which the chorus will read.

Staging

To help the chorus enhance the telling of this tale, have readers practice interjecting their sound effects words, and then have the speaker resume immediately. Strive for making this transition as smooth as possible.

Encore

You might wish to record your students' performance, and then have children use their puppets (see page 88) to act out the recorded story. They might enjoy creating a backdrop for the puppets, or adding a small bridge made of clay or cardboard.

Vocabulary

You may wish to introduce and discuss the following words before reading the script, or explain them during the first reading:

brook: a small stream, smaller than a river

gruff: rough or rude (this is also the goats' last name)

nibble: to eat by taking quick, small bites

Now Presenting...

The Three Billy Goats Gruff

After three billy goats outsmart a mean troll that lives under a bridge, they are able to enjoy the fresh green grass on the other side of the brook.

Characters

Storyteller .... _____

Little Billy Goat .... _____

Second Billy Goat .... _____

Big Billy Goat .... _____

Troll .... _____

Chorus .... _____

_____

_____

_____

 Readers' Theater, Grade 1 • EMC 3306

The Three Billy Goats Gruff

.... **Characters** ....

Storyteller   Big Billy Goat
Little Billy Goat   Troll
Second Billy Goat   Chorus

Storyteller: Long ago in a land of fresh green hills and bubbling brooks, there were three billy goats. Each day they nibbled the fresh green grass by the brook.

Chorus: Nibble, nibble, nibble.

Storyteller: One day, the three billy goats stood on their fresh green hill. As they looked across the bubbling brook, the little billy goat said…

Little Billy Goat: Look at the grass on the other side of the bubbling brook. It looks fresher. It looks greener. I'm going to cross the bridge and try it out.

Storyteller: The little billy goat trotted onto the bridge.

Chorus: Trip, trap, trip, trap.

Storyteller: Just as the little billy goat got to the center of the bridge, out jumped a mean, ugly troll.

Troll: Who's that trip, trap, trip, trapping on my bridge?

Little Billy Goat: It is I. I am Little Billy Goat Gruff. I'm crossing the bridge to try the fresh green grass on the other side of the bubbling brook.

Chorus: Bubble, bubble, bubble.

Troll: No one crosses my bridge! I am a mean, ugly troll, and I'm hungry, too. I'm going to eat you up!

Little Billy Goat: Oh, Mr. Troll, please don't eat me up! I'm just a little billy goat. You should wait for my big brother. He's much bigger than I am. I would be only a mouthful for you.

Storyteller: Now the troll looked at the little billy goat. That billy goat was small. That billy goat was thin.

Troll: Very well, then, Little Billy Goat. You go right along. I shall wait for your brother.

Storyteller: So the little billy goat trotted over the bridge.

Chorus: Trip, trap, trip, trap.

Storyteller: He nibbled the fresh green grass on the other side of the bubbling brook. Soon, the second billy goat got to thinking.

Second Billy Goat: I think the grass is greener over there. I'm going to cross the bridge and taste it.

Storyteller: So the second billy goat stepped onto the bridge.

Chorus: *(a little louder)* Trip, trap, trip, trap.

Storyteller: As the second billy goat got to the center of the bridge, out jumped the mean, ugly troll.

Troll: Who's that trip, trap, trip, trapping on my bridge?

Second Billy Goat: It is I. I am Second Billy Goat Gruff. I am crossing the bridge to try the fresh green grass on the other side of the bubbling brook.

Chorus: Bubble, bubble, bubble.

Troll: No one crosses my bridge! I am a mean, ugly troll, and I'm hungry, too. I'm going to eat you up!

Second Billy Goat: Oh, Mr. Troll, please don't eat me up! I'm a tough and stringy billy goat. I would be too hard to chew. You should wait for my big brother. He's tender and juicy.

Storyteller: Now the troll looked at the second billy goat. That billy goat looked tough. That billy goat looked stringy.

Troll: Very well, then, Second Billy Goat. I will wait for your brother.

Storyteller: So the second billy goat trotted over the bridge.

Chorus: Trip, trap, trip, trap.

Storyteller: He nibbled the fresh green grass on the other side of the bubbling brook. Soon, the big billy goat got to thinking.

Big Billy Goat: I think the grass is greener over there. I'm going to cross the bridge and taste it.

Storyteller: So the big billy goat stepped onto the bridge.

Chorus: *(even louder)* TRIP, TRAP, TRIP, TRAP.

Storyteller: Just as the big billy goat got to the center of the bridge, out jumped the mean, ugly troll.

Troll: Who's that TRIP, TRAP, TRIP, TRAPPING on my bridge?

Big Billy Goat: It is I. I am Big Billy Goat Gruff. I am crossing the bridge to try the fresh green grass on the other side of the bubbling brook.

Chorus: Bubble, bubble, bubble.

Troll: No one crosses my bridge! I am a mean, ugly troll, and I'm going to eat you up!

Big Billy Goat: Oh, Mr. Troll, please let me join my brothers on the other side of the bridge.

Storyteller: Now the troll looked at the big billy goat. He rubbed his chin.

Troll: I let Little Billy Goat cross the bridge because he was too small and too thin. I let Second Billy Goat cross the bridge because he was too tough and too stringy. You are not small and thin. You are not tough and stringy. You look tender and juicy. I am going to eat you up!

Big Billy Goat: Don't be so sure, Mr. Troll! Remember, we are the billy goats Gruff!

Storyteller: The big billy goat looked at the troll and smiled his big billy goat smile. Then he put down his head and knocked the troll right into the bubbling brook!

Chorus: Bubble, bubble, bubble.

Storyteller: Then Big Billy Goat trotted over the bridge. He nibbled the fresh green grass with his brothers. And that's the last anyone ever heard of the mean, ugly troll.

Chorus: Bubble, bubble, bubble!

Gruff Words

Draw a line to connect each word to the correct billy goat Gruff.

tough

juicy

tender

small

thin

medium

stringy

large

Stick Puppets

Color the puppets. Cut them out and tape them to a straw or craft stick. Use the puppets to tell the story. Work with a group.

Now Presenting...

The Little Red Hen

This timeless tale reminds children that nobody likes to be stuck doing all the work all the time!

Setting the Stage

Background

Discuss with students the process of making bread. Ask questions such as:

Where does bread come from? How is it made? Who are the people who do the work of making bread? What other kinds of helpful work do people do?

Staging

Place the student playing Little Red Hen at center stage, with the "lazy" animal friends scattered around her. Consider providing real bread that can be shared among students after the lesson.

Vocabulary

Introduce and discuss the following words before reading the script:

cottage: a small house

flour: a fine powder made by grinding wheat; used for baking and cooking

grain: the seed of wheat or other cereal grasses

grind: to crush into bits or powder

harvest: to cut and gather in wheat or other grain crops

mill: a machine for grinding grain into flour

pond: a body of still water; a pond is smaller than a lake

porch: a covered entrance to a building

wheat: the grain produced by a type of cereal grass

The Little Red Hen

Work is much easier when it is shared. Learn how Little Red Hen tries to teach her friends this important lesson.

Characters

Narrator 1 .... _____

Narrator 2 .... _____

Little Red Hen................... _____

Pig .... _____

Dog.................................... _____

Cat..................................... _____

Duck .... _____

Baby Chicks .... _____

_____

_____

The Little Red Hen

.... **Characters** ....

Narrator 1	Dog
Narrator 2	Cat
Little Red Hen	Duck
Pig	Baby Chicks

Narrator 1: Once there was a tiny cottage in the country.

Narrator 2: In the cottage on a farm, there once lived a little red hen and her baby chicks. Her friends lived with her on the farm.

Narrator 1: Her friends were a dog, a duck, a cat, and a pig.

Narrator 2: Little Red Hen was a very hard worker. She kept the house, cared for the garden, and cooked food for her chicks and her friends.

Narrator 1: The friends, however, were very lazy.

Pig: I like to roll around in the mud all day.

Dog: I like to lie around in the shade all day.

Cat: I like to nap on the porch all day.

Duck: I like to float around on the pond all day.

Narrator 2: One day, Little Red Hen was sweeping the front yard when she found a few grains of wheat.

Little Red Hen: Who will help me plant this wheat?

Pig: Not I! I have to roll around in the mud.

Dog: Not I! I have to lie here in the shade.

Cat: Not I! I have to finish my nap.

Duck: Not I! I'm busy floating.

Little Red Hen: Very well then. I will plant the wheat myself.

Baby Chicks: And so she did.

Narrator 1: The wheat grew and grew. Soon it was ripe and ready to harvest.

Little Red Hen: Who will help me harvest the wheat?

Pig: Not I! I have to roll around in the mud.

Dog: Not I! I have to lie here in the shade.

Cat: Not I! I have to finish my nap.

Duck: Not I! I'm busy floating.

Little Red Hen: Very well then. I will harvest the wheat myself.

Baby Chicks: And so she did.

Narrator 2: Now the wheat was ready to be ground into flour.

Little Red Hen: Who will take the wheat to the miller and ask him to grind it into flour for us?

Pig: Not I! I have to roll around in the mud.

Dog: Not I! I have to lie here in the shade.

Cat: Not I! I have to finish my nap.

Duck: Not I! I'm busy floating.

Little Red Hen: Very well then. I will take the wheat to the miller myself.

Baby Chicks: And so she did.

Narrator 1: The little red hen came home from the mill with a plump sack full of flour.

Little Red Hen: Who will help me make bread with this flour?

Pig: Not I! I have to roll around in the mud.

Dog: Not I! I have to lie here in the shade.

Cat: Not I! I have to finish my nap.

Duck: Not I! I'm busy floating.

Little Red Hen: Very well then. I will bake the bread myself.

Baby Chicks: And so she did.

Narrator 2: Soon the wonderful smell of baking bread filled the air.

Narrator 1: Cat, Dog, Duck, and Pig gathered around as Little Red Hen took two beautiful brown loaves out of the oven.

Narrator 2: They licked their lips as Little Red Hen placed the loaves on the table.

Narrator 1: Their eyes gleamed as she set out a crock of sweet butter and a pot of raspberry jam.

Narrator 2: When everything was ready, Little Red Hen called to her friends.

Little Red Hen: Who will help me eat the bread?

Pig: I will!

Dog: I will!

Cat: I will!

Duck: I will!

Little Red Hen: Oh no, you won't! I planted the wheat. I harvested the wheat. I took the wheat to the mill to be ground into flour. I brought the flour home to bake the bread. My little chicks and I will eat the bread!

Baby Chicks: And so we did.

Narrator 1: From that day forward, Cat, Dog, Pig, and Duck tried to be a little more helpful.

Name _____

Action Words

Words that show action are called **verbs**. Draw a picture to illustrate each verb from the story.

sweep	**plant**
harvest	**bake**

Name _____

No, You Won't!

1. Why did Little Red Hen decide not to share the bread with her friends?

_____

_____

_____

_____

_____

2. Do you think she made the right decision? Explain.

_____

_____

_____

_____

_____

Now Presenting...

Shapes in the City

Shapes are all around us. Come take a stroll through the city streets and find circles, triangles, squares, rectangles, and octagons.

Setting the Stage

Background

To begin a discussion of shapes, ask children to mention the shapes they know and to point out items they can see in the classroom that exemplify each shape. Help them articulate the characteristics of each with simple descriptions such as, "A square has four straight sides that are all the same length." Be sure children are familiar with circles, triangles, squares, rectangles, and octagons before reading the script.

Staging

Cut out a circle, square, rectangle, triangle, and octagon from posterboard. Punch a hole in each shape and string it on a length of yarn. Each of the readers playing the part of a shape can wear one of these "shape necklaces."

Vocabulary

You may wish to introduce and discuss the following words before reading the script, or explain them during the first reading:

circle: a round line

corner: a place where two lines meet

octagon: a figure with eight angles and eight sides

rectangle: a figure with four angles and four sides

round: shaped like a ball or circle

square: a figure with four equal sides and four right (equal) angles

triangle: a figure with three angles and three sides

Shapes in the City

Take a walk through the streets of a city and look for all kinds of shapes.

Characters

Narrator 1 .... _____

Narrator 2 .... _____

Circle .... _____

Square.............................. _____

Triangle .... _____

Rectangle .... _____

Octagon............................ _____

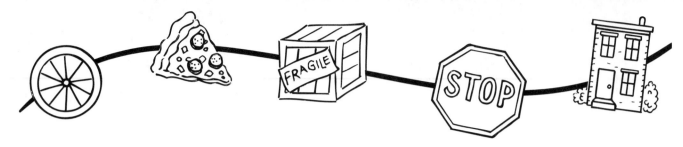

Shapes in the City

·················· **Characters** ··················

Narrator 1	Triangle
Narrator 2	Rectangle
Circle	Octagon
Square	

Narrator 1: There are lots of shapes to be seen in the city!

Narrator 2: Here are our friends, the shapes, to tell you more about it.

Circle: There are circles in the city!

Square: And squares!

Triangle: And triangles!

Rectangle: And rectangles!

Octagon: And don't forget the really fun shapes—like me, the octagon!

Narrator 1: Let's join the shapes on their walk through the busy city.

Circle: Circles are everywhere. Do you see circles in bus wheels and taxi wheels?

Square: Yes, and in bicycle wheels, too!

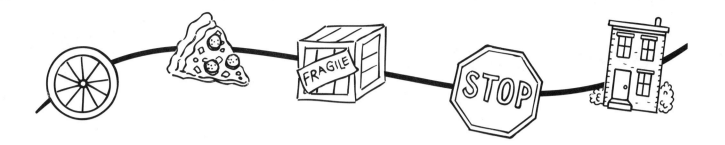

Rectangle: Hey, look! There goes a guy on roller blades. Those wheels are small circles, too.

Circle: Check out those stoplights. Red, yellow, and green circles. Beautiful!

Square: Okay, Circle. I have to admit it. You really **do** get around!

Octagon: Get a-ROUND! That's a good one, Square!

All: *(laughing)*

Rectangle: I think Square and I are actually the shapes you see most often. I mean, look at these buildings!

Square: He's right!

Rectangle: Everywhere you look there are squares and rectangles. Windows, doors, walls—even the sidewalks are made of rectangles and squares!

Circle: Bricks and tiles are made of squares and rectangles, too.

Triangle: And look at the boxes in the back of that truck. They are all full of squares and rectangles.

Octagon: The books and magazines in the library are rectangles, too!

Square: *(sighing)* Corners, lovely right angle corners. The city is just full of them!

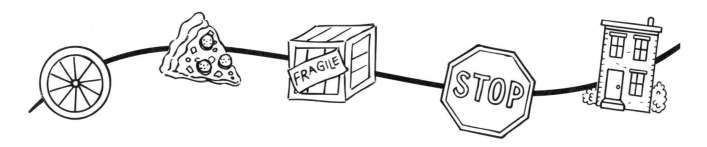

Triangle: You guys aren't the only ones with corners, you know! I have corners, too.

Octagon: Yeah, but just three! I have eight!

Triangle: Three is pretty cool, though. Look at the peaks on those rooftops! Look at that bright yellow traffic sign.

Circle: I see some triangles on that bridge.

Triangle: Bridges are often made of triangles. Do you know why?

Rectangle: Haven't got a clue!

Triangle: Because triangles are strong shapes— that's why!

Octagon: I'm a pretty strong shape myself!

Square: How's that?

Octagon: I can stop a great big city bus! I can stop a huge dump truck! I can do it, really I can!

Rectangle: You can't do that! You're just a shape.

Octagon: Oh, yeah? Come on down to the corner, and I'll prove it.

Narrator 2: The shapes walked down the street until they came to a corner that was marked with...

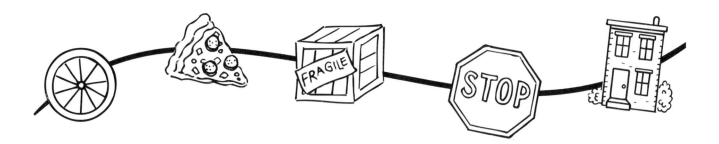

Circle: ... a stop sign!

Rectangle: It's an octagon!

Narrator 1: Just at that moment, an enormous truck comes to a stop right in front of the shapes. A taxi stops, too. So does a garbage truck.

Octagon: You see! You see!

Rectangle: That **is** pretty impressive, Octagon.

Square: There may not be as many of you as there are of me, but I have to admit that you are quite important!

Octagon: Thank you, Square. And really, don't you think red is my color?

All: *(laughing)*

Circle: I have to admit, it's hard to imagine a purple stop sign.

Triangle: I'm getting hungry.

Rectangle: Me, too.

Square: What do you want for lunch, everyone?

Triangle: *(smiling)* Circle and I know a great pizza place. Come on, shapes, let's get rolling!

Circle Search

Draw a circle around each object that has the shape of a **circle**.

Name _____

Your Favorite Shape

Write the name of each shape.

circle	octagon	rectangle
triangle	square	

_____

_____

_____

_____

_____

Use your favorite shape
to draw a picture.

Name _____

Shape Search

Circle the shape words hidden in this word search. Cross off the words in the list as you find them.

Shape Words				
angle	big	circle	line	little
octagon	rectangle	round	square	triangle

```
t  r  e  c  t  a  n  g  l  e
r  o  w  i  r  t  a  o  e  k
i  c  i  r  c  l  e  l  a  l
a  r  u  b  o  s  x  i  v  i
n  o  d  r  y  l  i  n  i  t
g  u  b  i  g  n  a  e  s  t
l  n  o  c  t  a  g  o  n  l
e  d  r  i  h  s  r  y  o  e
w  a  n  g  l  e  l  u  x  r
q  s  q  u  a  r  e  x  y  n
```

Now Presenting...

Taxi the Turtle

Squirt the Squirrel learns an important lesson about kindness and friendship.

7 parts

Program................. page 108

Script ....pages 109–113

Activities .... pages 114 & 115

Setting the Stage

Background

Encourage children to talk about what it means to be a good friend to others. Ask children how they feel when people tease or make fun of them. Tell them that in this script, one of the characters learns that taking time to be kind to others can really make a difference!

Encore

Have children use the pictures on page 115 to retell the story to a partner, or send the activity home for children to tell the story to a family member.

Vocabulary

You may wish to introduce and discuss the following words before reading the script, or explain them during the first reading:

apologize: to say you are sorry

brag: to boast or show off about yourself and what you can do

budge: to move someone or something

give a lift: offer a ride to somebody

slowpoke: somebody who does everything very slowly

willing: when you don't mind doing something

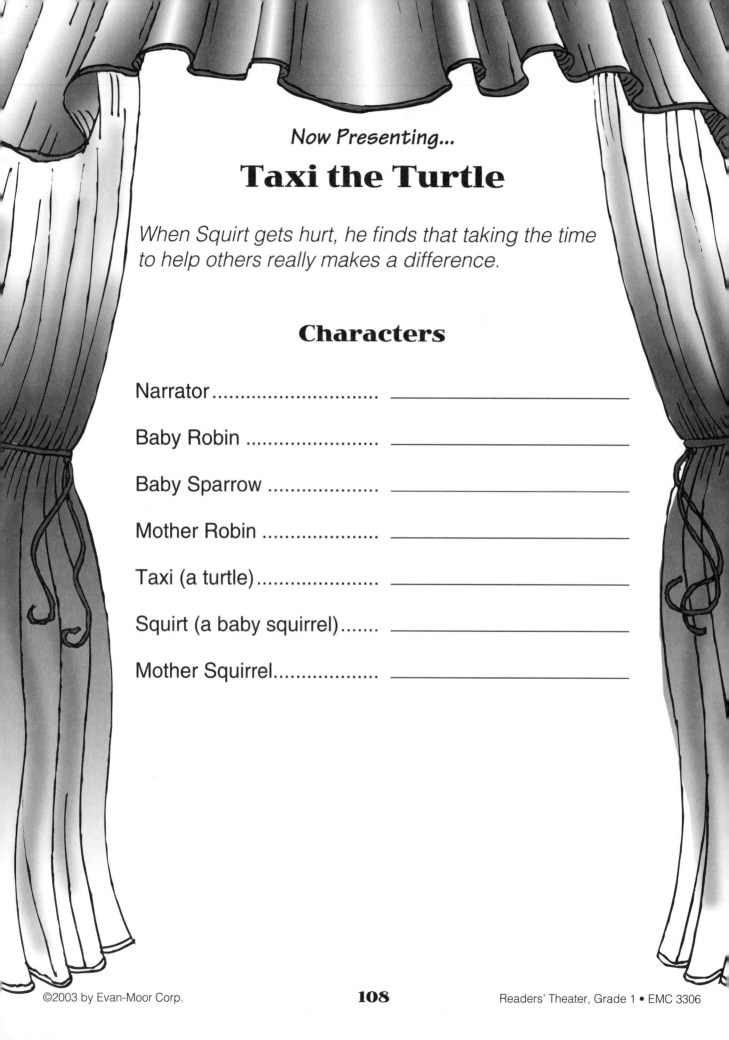

Now Presenting...

Taxi the Turtle

When Squirt gets hurt, he finds that taking the time to help others really makes a difference.

Characters

Narrator .... _____

Baby Robin .... _____

Baby Sparrow .... _____

Mother Robin .... _____

Taxi (a turtle) .... _____

Squirt (a baby squirrel)....... _____

Mother Squirrel.................. _____

 Readers' Theater, Grade 1 • EMC 3306

Taxi the Turtle

········· **Characters** ·········

Narrator	Taxi
Baby Robin	Squirt
Baby Sparrow	Mother Squirrel
Mother Robin	

Baby Robin: Chirp, chirp! Thank you, Taxi.

Baby Sparrow: Yes, Taxi. Thanks so much!

Narrator: The two little birds hopped off the back of a big turtle. The turtle, Taxi, had just carried them home from their music lessons.

Mother Robin: Thank you, Taxi. I never worry about where my baby is when you are in charge. You are such a big help.

Taxi: I like to help out when I can, Mrs. Robin.

Mother Robin: Oh, and Mrs. Sparrow asked me to give you this fresh clover from Sunny Meadow. She's still out on her errands, so Baby Sparrow will stay here with us. But Mrs. Sparrow wanted me to be sure to thank you for bringing her baby home, too.

Taxi: Yum. That looks fresh and tasty! How nice of Mrs. Sparrow to think of me!

Narrator: Mrs. Sparrow and Mrs. Robin are not the only grateful mothers. All the mothers in Friendly Forest love Taxi. He is always happy to help.

Baby Robin: Taxi carries all the baby birds that are too young to fly.

Baby Sparrow: He also gives a lift to little chipmunks and bunnies who get tired out after a long day of running and jumping.

Mother Robin: Everyone loves Taxi because he is always willing to help.

Squirt: That's not true! I don't love Taxi! I think he's a slowpoke! I would never take a ride on Taxi!

Narrator: Well, as you see, everyone in Friendly Forest loves Taxi, except for Squirt the Squirrel.

Squirt: That's right! Who needs a turtle anyway? He's so slow. I could crawl faster than Taxi's fastest walk!

Baby Robin: Oh, Taxi, don't listen to Squirt. He just likes to brag.

Taxi: Well, it hurts my feelings when Squirt makes fun of me. I may be slow, but I can still help others.

Mother Robin: Of course you can, Taxi. Squirt is missing out on having a good friend by being mean to you!

Narrator: Then one day, Squirt hurt himself when he was playing in Friendly Forest.

Squirt: Help! Somebody come give me a hand!

Narrator: Baby Robin and Baby Sparrow fluttered over when they heard the noise.

Baby Sparrow: What's going on, Squirt? Is this a game you're playing?

Squirt: No, I mean it! I just stepped into Mr. Chipmunk's tunnel and turned my ankle. You've got to help me!

Baby Robin: Well, we can't exactly give you a hand. But we'll try to help you get out of there.

Narrator: Try as they might, though, the baby birds could not budge Squirt. Finally, Baby Robin went to get his mother while Baby Sparrow stayed with Squirt.

Mother Robin: Oh, dear. You're in quite a fix, Squirt. You need someone stronger than a bird to help you.

Baby Robin: Look! There goes Taxi! It looks like he's already got something on his back.

Baby Sparrow: I'll go talk to him.

Squirt: Taxi won't help me. Not after all the mean things I've said to him.

Mother Robin: Now, Squirt. Taxi is one of the kindest animals in the forest. I'm sure he'll be happy to help you after you apologize to him.

Squirt: You mean I have to say I'm sorry?

Mother Robin: Well, it sure sounded like you were sorry just a moment ago.

Squirt: You're right. I guess I can do this.

Narrator: Just then, Taxi walked up. Baby Sparrow sat on a long branch tied to Taxi's back with a vine.

Taxi: Baby Sparrow told me what happened, Squirt. I was just taking this branch over to the Critter Kids' Playground to make a seesaw. But I guess I can do that later if you need help.

Squirt: Taxi, you are such a good friend. I'm sorry I made fun of you and said all those mean things to you. I really am.

Taxi: Thank you, Squirt. I knew you weren't really mean. I guess it's just that you're always in such a big hurry.

Squirt: And look what happened to me because of it! My ankle really hurts! I guess this will slow me down.

Taxi: Well, let's stop all this talk and get you out of here!

Narrator: Mother Robin and the baby birds helped settle Squirt on Taxi's back. Soon, Taxi delivered Squirt to his tree.

Squirt: Thanks, Taxi. I never would have made it without you.

Mother Squirrel: Squirt! What on earth happened?

Squirt: It's nothing, Mama. I just twisted my ankle. My friend Taxi gave me a ride home.

Mother Squirrel: That was kind of you, Taxi. What a good friend.

Taxi: Aw, that's OK. I like to help out when I can.

Squirt: Taxi, as soon as my ankle is better, I'd love to help you set up that seesaw over at the playground.

Taxi: That would be great, Squirt.

Squirt: I think I'd like to try helping out when I can, too!

Taxi: I have a feeling you're going to like it!

Name _____

Acts of Kindness

Taxi did many kind things. Draw a picture of one of the kind things he did. Then write about it.

_____

_____

_____

_____

Tell the Story

Color the pictures and cut them out. Glue them in the correct order on another sheet of paper. Then tell the story.

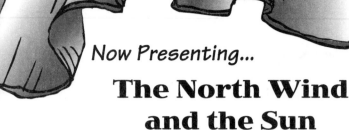

Now Presenting...

The North Wind and the Sun

In this ancient fable, the North Wind and the Sun compete to find out which one can make a pair of travelers remove their coats. The North Wind uses brute force, while the Sun tries a gentler approach.

Setting the Stage

Background

Guide children in a discussion of the weather. Ask children to think about which cardinal direction (north, south, east, or west) is most associated with cold weather. You may wish to point out the Arctic Circle at the top of a globe or map and tell students that the North Wind, which blows down out of the north, is a blustery and cold wind.

Staging

Provide coats for the children who read the parts of the travelers in the story.

Vocabulary

You may wish to introduce and discuss the following words before reading the script, or explain them during the first reading:

blast: to send a sharp gust of wind

bluster: to blow with great force

contest: a competition to see who will win

feeble: not strong

gale: a powerful wind

Now Presenting...

The North Wind and the Sun

The North Wind and the Sun compete to see who can force two travelers to remove their coats.

Characters

Narrator 1 .... _____

Narrator 2 .... _____

North Wind........................ _____

Sun .... _____

Man.................................... _____

Woman .... _____

Chorus .... _____

_____

_____

_____

The North Wind and the Sun

······················ **Characters** ·····················

Narrator 1   Man
Narrator 2   Woman
North Wind   Chorus
Sun

Narrator 1: One morning two travelers walked up a dusty mountain road.

Narrator 2: The Sun and the North Wind sat high in the clouds, watching.

North Wind: Look at those silly people down there. They are so weak and small.

Sun: Yes, they are little. But they look happy.

Narrator 1: And it was true. The two were laughing and singing as they walked along.

North Wind: Ha! Why are they so happy? Don't they know that they are feeble and weak? I am much stronger than they are!

Sun: You are stronger than those travelers, North Wind. But I am stronger than you are.

North Wind: You are not! I can bluster. I can blast. I can blow the ice and snow wherever I choose! I am stronger!

Sun: Hmm. Let's have a contest. Let's see which of us can make those travelers remove their coats.

North Wind: Ha, ha! I shall win easily.

Sun: Go ahead, then. You go first.

Chorus: The sky grew dark. The air grew cold. The North Wind puffed up his cheeks and he blew. He blew and blew and blew.

Man: My, what a cold wind all of a sudden!

Narrator 2: The traveler buttoned his coat tightly from top to bottom.

Woman: I'm starting to shiver!

Narrator 1: The woman zipped her coat tightly from bottom to top.

North Wind: I am stronger than buttons or zippers. How do you like this?

Chorus: The sky grew darker. The air grew colder. The North Wind puffed up his cheeks and he blew. He blew and blew and blew.

Man: This is quite a gale.

Narrator 2: The man tightened the belt on his coat.

Woman: Yes, isn't it exciting?

Narrator 1: The woman folded her arms across her chest.

Narrator 2: This made the North Wind very mad. He took a deep breath.

Chorus: Then the sky grew darker than dark. The air grew colder than cold. The North Wind puffed up his cheeks and he blew. He blew and blew and blew.

Narrator 1: Dust swirled around the travelers. Leaves were snatched from the trees.

Narrator 2: Drops of ice fell down from the sky. But the man and the woman just snuggled deeper into their coats.

Narrator 1: The North Wind was very, very mad. But he was also very tired.

Sun: Now it's my turn.

North Wind: You saw what happened! It's too difficult. You can't do it!

Sun: Well, I shall give it a try.

Chorus: The sky turned a sweet shade of blue. The air grew warm. The Sun shone softly on the travelers.

Man: Oh, what a lovely bit of sunshine.

Narrator 2: The man loosened his belt.

Woman: Indeed! It feels wonderful.

Narrator 1: The woman raised her arms to the Sun. She did a little dance.

Narrator 2: The Sun smiled.

Chorus: The sky turned a sweeter shade of blue. The air grew warmer. The Sun shone gently on the two travelers.

Man: Ah, how delightful.

Narrator 1: The man unbuttoned his coat from bottom to top.

Woman: It's heavenly.

Narrator 2: The woman unzipped her coat from top to bottom. The pair began to sing again.

North Wind: Humph! What a bunch of nonsense. See, they still have their coats on.

Sun: Not for long!

Chorus: Then the sky turned a shade of blue that was sweeter than sweet. The air grew warmer than warm. The Sun shone brightly on the two travelers.

Man: I am too warm.

Woman: Me, too! I do not need this heavy coat.

Narrator 1: The two travelers took off their coats. They put the coats into their packs.

Sun: Ho, ho, North Wind! I did it!

North Wind: I can hardly believe it! Your gentleness was more powerful than my strength!

Name _____

Opposites

Draw a line to match each word to its opposite.

loose	cold
weak	strong
hot	happy
zip	powerful
difficult	top
bottom	easy
sad	tight
gentle	unzip

Draw a picture to illustrate one pair of opposites from this page.

On another sheet of paper, write down as many pairs of opposites as you can. Work with a friend or by yourself.

 Readers' Theater, Grade 1 • EMC 3306

Name _____

A Warm, Sunny Day

The travelers in the story enjoyed the warm sunshine. Draw a picture and write a sentence to tell what you like to do on a warm, sunny day.

Now Presenting...

Elephants
in the Wild

Joyce Poole, a famous elephant scientist, visits a classroom to teach children about elephants in the wild.

7 parts

Program................. page 126

Script ....pages 127–131

Activities .... pages 132 & 133

Setting the Stage

Background

Joyce Poole spent more than 15 years studying elephants in Kenya. Help students locate Kenya in East Africa on a globe or map. Explain that this is one of several areas in the world where elephants live. If possible, display photos of elephants in the wild.

Staging

Arrange readers in a circle around Joyce. The narrator introduces the vignette, then moves offstage.

Vocabulary

You may wish to introduce and discuss the following words before reading the script, or explain them during the first reading:

bark: a short, sharp sound, like the noise made by a dog

crush: to make something collapse under heavy weight

grunt: a deep, hoarse sound

rumble: a deep, heavy, ongoing sound

squeal: to make a long, shrill cry

trumpet: to make a loud sound, like the kind made by a trumpet

trunk: the long, flexible snout of an elephant

wild: living untamed in a forest or jungle

Now Presenting...

Elephants in the Wild

Scientist Joyce Poole talks with children about her lifelong work with elephants.

Characters

Narrator............................. _____

Joyce Poole .... _____

Students:

   Robby............................ _____

   Sima.............................. _____

   Ramon .... _____

   Karim............................. _____

   Tracy .... _____

Elephants in the Wild

············ **Characters** ············

Narrator   Ramon
Joyce Poole   Karim
Robby   Tracy
Sima

Narrator: Joyce Poole is an elephant expert. Today she is visiting a first-grade class that is learning about elephants.

Joyce: Good morning, everyone.

Students: Good morning!

Joyce: Let me tell you a little bit about myself. I was born in America but I grew up in Africa.

Robby: Why?

Joyce: My father worked for the Peace Corps. He worked in Kenya, which is a country in Africa.

Sima: Do elephants live there?

Joyce: Yes, they do.

Ramon: How did you start studying elephants?

Joyce: I went to college and studied biology. Then I came back to Africa to study elephants.

Karim: Did you live in a tent?

Joyce: Yes, most of the time I did.

Tracy: That must have been fun.

Joyce: I liked it, but it was not easy.

Robby: Why not?

Joyce: Well, it was often very hot. It was dirty, and there were lots of bugs and things.

Sima: Was it dangerous?

Joyce: Yes. There were lots of wild animals. We had to be careful. Once a tree fell right on my tent and crushed it! Luckily, I wasn't there at the time.

Karim: How do you study an elephant?

Joyce: First, you have to find the elephants. Then you have to sit and watch what they do. You write everything down in a notebook.

Tracy: What did you find out?

Joyce: We learned many, many things.

Robby: Like what?

Joyce: We learned that elephants talk to each other.

Sima: Elephants can't talk!

Joyce: They don't use words like we do, but they really can talk to each other.

Ramon: How?

Joyce: They use many different kinds of sounds. They grunt. They squeal. They trumpet. They even bark!

Karim: That's funny.

Joyce: Some of the sounds they make **are** funny. And some of the sounds are too low for our ears to hear.

Tracy: Can other elephants hear them?

Joyce: Yes. Sometimes they can hear sounds even if they are miles away.

Ramon: What else did you learn?

Joyce: We learned that elephants have families, and that they care about each other.

Robby: How do you know?

Joyce: Elephants stay together in family groups. The females work together to take care of the babies.

Sima: What else do they do?

Joyce: They make a lot of happy fuss when they greet each other. They flap their ears and make a rumbling noise.

Karim: Do they shake hands?

Joyce: *(laughing)* No, they don't shake hands. But they **do** pet each other with their trunks.

Tracy: Do you really believe they have feelings?

Joyce: Yes, I am sure they do. When they find the bones of a dead elephant, they sometimes try to bury them. They kick dirt over the bones. They break off branches and place them over the bones.

Ramon: Wow!

Joyce: And they get really sad when a family member dies. Their ears droop. Their bodies sag. They don't have any energy. They don't play.

Tracy: How long do elephants live?

Joyce: Many elephants live to be 50 or 60 years old.

Ramon: What do they eat?

Joyce: They eat grass and leaves.

Sima: How do they drink?

Joyce: They suck water into their trunks. Then they spray the water into their mouths.

Karim: I'd sure like to see elephants in the wild!

Robby: Me, too!

Joyce: Maybe someday you can all come and visit me in Africa!

Elephant Words

Write a list of words that tell about this elephant. Then use some of your words to write a sentence about the elephant.

_____   _____   _____

_____   _____   _____

_____

_____

The Biggest Elephant

Circle the biggest elephant in each row.

Now Presenting...

The Three Little Pigs

This traditional tale includes a moral about the value of slow, careful work.

Setting the Stage

Background

Encourage children to summarize the plot of this story. Before they hear the script for the first time, tell them to listen to the moral—or lesson—at the end of the story.

You might use a book such as Ann Morris's photo-illustrated *Houses and Homes* to show children images of houses made of various materials including straw, twigs or sticks, and bricks.

Staging

Encourage the readers taking the parts of the three pigs to develop a dance sequence to accompany their refrain: "We're the three little pigs. Pigs, pigs, jiggity jig. We're the three little pigs." They might incorporate stepping and stomping, and turning and bowing.

Encore

Children may enjoy reading other versions of this tale, such as Paul Galdone's traditional version, *The Three Little Pigs*, or Jon Scieszka's *The True Story of the Three Little Pigs*, told from the wolf's perspective.

Vocabulary

Introduce and discuss the following words before reading the script:

straw: the stalk or stem of dry grain plants

twig: a small branch

The Three Little Pigs

When three little pigs build their own homes, the materials they choose and the care they use make all the difference in the world!

Characters

Narrator .... _____

Mother Pig .... _____

Pig 1 .... _____

Pig 2 .... _____

Pig 3 .... _____

Farmer .... _____

Woodsman .... _____

Builder .... _____

Big Bad Wolf...................... _____

The Three Little Pigs

.... **Characters** ....

Narrator	Farmer
Mother Pig	Woodsman
Pig 1	Builder
Pig 2	Big Bad Wolf
Pig 3	

Narrator: Once upon a time there were three little pigs.

Pigs 1, 2, & 3: We're the three little pigs. Pigs, pigs, jiggity jig. We're the three little pigs.

Narrator: The three little pigs had lived at home with their mother for some time. But when they got older, Mother Pig said:

Mother Pig: My little pigs, it is time for you to go out into the great big world. Pack up your things!

Narrator: So the three little pigs packed up their things, kissed their mother good-bye, and started off down the road.

Pigs 1, 2, & 3: We're the three little pigs. Pigs, pigs, jiggity jig. We're the three little pigs.

Pig 1: We're all alone, out in the big world!

Pig 2: Where will we stay?

Pig 3: Look! Here comes a farmer with a wagon full of straw!

Pig 1: Good day, Mr. Farmer. May I please have some straw? I will build a house of straw.

Farmer: Here is a bundle of straw for you, my fine fellow.

Pig 1: Thank you, kind sir. My brothers, I shall stop here to build my house. Farewell.

Pigs 2 & 3: Pigs, pigs, jiggity jig. Now we're just two little pigs.

Narrator: So the first little pig stopped and built a house of straw while his brothers went on down the road. After a while, they met a woodsman with a load of twigs.

Pig 2: Good day, Mr. Woodsman. May I please have some twigs? I will build a house of twigs.

Woodsman: Here is a bundle of twigs for you, my fine fellow.

Pig 2: Thank you, kind sir. My brother, I shall stop here to build my house. Farewell.

Pig 3: Pig, pig, jiggity jig. Now I'm just one little pig.

Narrator: So the second little pig stopped and built a house of twigs while his brother went on down the road. After a while, he met a builder with a cart full of bricks.

Pig 3: Good day, Mr. Builder. May I please have some bricks? I will build my house of bricks.

Builder: Here is a stack of bricks for you, my fine fellow.

Pig 3: Thank you, kind sir. I shall stop here to build my house.

Narrator: Now, the first little pig and the second little pig had built their houses very quickly.

Pigs 1 & 2: Snip, snap—as fast as that!

Narrator: The third little pig worked slowly and carefully. He put the bricks together one at a time.

Pig 3: Slow and steady—carefully. My house is as strong as it can be!

Narrator: Now the three little pigs each had a new house right in the same neighborhood. Soon, the big bad wolf decided to visit his new neighbors.

Wolf: Heh-heh-heh. I'm feeling SO hungry today. Maybe one of my juicy, new little neighbors would like to invite me in for a tasty bite or two.

Narrator: So the wolf knocked on the door of the little straw house.

Wolf: Heh-heh-heh. Oh, little pig, little pig! Let me come in.

Pig 1: Not by the hair on my chinny-chin-chin.

Wolf: Then I'll huff and I'll puff and I'll blow your house in!

Narrator: So the wolf huffed. *(blowing)* And the wolf puffed. *(blowing harder)* And the wolf blew the house down. *(blowing even harder)*

Pig 1: Oh no! Where will I go?

Narrator: The little pig ran to his brother's house of twigs.

Wolf: Heh-heh-heh. Two pigs are better than one. I'll try this house next.

Narrator: So the wolf knocked on the door of the little twig house.

Wolf: Heh-heh-heh. Oh, little pigs, little pigs! Let me come in.

Pigs 1 & 2: Not by the hair on our chinny-chin-chins.

Wolf: Then I'll huff and I'll puff and I'll blow your house in!

Narrator: So the wolf huffed. *(blowing)* And the wolf puffed. *(blowing harder)* And the wolf blew the house down. *(blowing even harder)*

Pigs 1 & 2: Oh no! Where will we go?

Narrator: The two little pigs ran to their brother's house of bricks.

Wolf: Heh-heh-heh. Three little pigs are better than two. I'll try this house next.

Narrator: And the wolf knocked on the door of the little brick house.

Wolf: Heh-heh-heh. Oh, little pigs, little pigs! Let me come in.

Pigs 1, 2, & 3: Not by the hair on our chinny-chin-chins.

Wolf: Then I'll huff and I'll puff and I'll blow your house in!

Narrator: So the wolf huffed. *(blowing)* And the wolf puffed. *(blowing harder)* And the wolf huffed again. *(blowing even harder)* But the brick house didn't budge!

All: And the moral of this story is:
If you're going to make something
and you want it to last,
it's better to make it carefully
than to make it fast!

Pigs: *(quietly)* Pigs, pigs, jiggity jig.

Wolf: Heh-heh-heh.

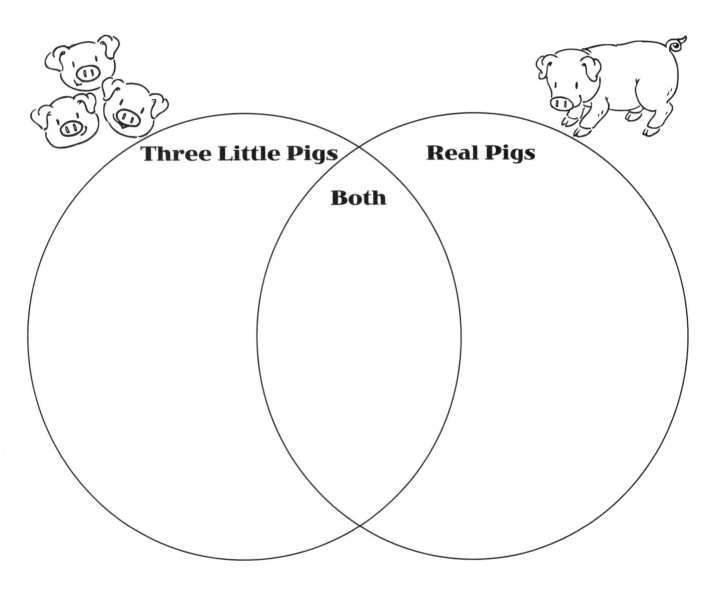

Real and Make-Believe

Which words describe the pigs in the story? Which words describe real pigs? Which words describe both? Copy the words into the correct part of this Venn diagram.

Three Little Pigs

Real Pigs

Both

| they can do a jig | they can run | they can talk |
| they are plump | they build houses | they roll in mud |

Words with -ig

Write the words. Then use the words to complete the sentences below.

b + ig = _____ _____ _____

d + ig = _____ _____ _____

j + ig = _____ _____ _____

tw + ig = _____ _____ _____ _____

1. The pigs danced a little _____.

2. A _____ is a little branch.

3. _____ is the opposite of **little**.

4. Will you _____ a little hole for me?

Draw a picture of a big pig holding a twig and doing a jig.

Answer Key

Why Bear Has a Stumpy Tail

Page 15: Pictures should show the appropriate tail for each animal.; 1) bear; 2) mouse; 3) fox; 4) rabbit

Page 16: From upper left corner, clockwise: groundhog, fox, rabbit, bear, mouse, fish

Math at Farmers' Market

Page 24: 1) $6.25 (currency selection may vary); 2) $3.50 (currency selection may vary); 3) $4.50 (currency selection may vary)

Page 25: Answers will vary, but should be reasonable considering the amount of money designated.

Stagecoach Mary

Page 33: Drawings will vary. Sentences should describe Mary delivering mail.

Page 34:

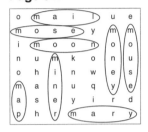

All Through the Year

Page 42: Answers will vary. Pictures should be appropriate to the season and labeled correctly.

Page 43: 1) 2 + 3 + 1 = 6; 2) 2 + 2 + 1 + 1 = 6; 3) 3 + 3 = 6; 4) 1 + 1 + 1 + 1 + 2 = 6

Too Much Noise!

Page 51: The names of the animals should be matched with the correct pictures. Drawings will vary.

Page 52: poking; bawling; knocking; hatching; braying

The Shark King's Son

Page 60: Drawings will vary, but should be appropriate to each word given.

Page 61: 1) happy; 2) worried; 3) sad; 4) surprised; 5) angry; 6) afraid

Out in the Woods

Page 69:

Example: The bear is hiding behind the big rock.

Page 70: The names of the senses and body parts should be matched correctly.; I hear with my <u>ears</u>.; I see with my <u>eyes</u>.; I smell with my <u>nose</u>.; I taste with my <u>mouth</u>.; I touch with my <u>hand</u>.

Big Mose

Page 78: Drawings will vary, but should be appropriate for the sounds of the words given.

Page 79: Drawings and sentences will vary.

The Three Billy Goats Gruff

Page 87: second billy goat—tough, stringy, medium; **little billy goat**—small, thin; **big billy goat**—juicy, tender, large

The Little Red Hen

Page 96: Drawings will vary. Pictures should convey the meanings of the verbs.

Page 97: 1) Possible answer: Little Red Hen decided not to share the bread with her friends because they did not help her plant the wheat, harvest the wheat, or bake the bread when she asked them to.; 2) Answers will vary.

Shapes in the City

Page 104:

Page 105: Check for correct labeling of shapes. Drawings will vary.

Page 106:

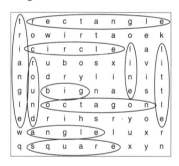

Taxi the Turtle

Page 114: Pictures and writing will vary.

Page 115:

The North Wind and the Sun

Page 123: loose–tight, weak–strong, hot–cold, zip–unzip, difficult–easy, bottom–top, sad–happy, gentle–powerful
Rest of answers will vary.

Page 124: Drawings and sentences will vary. Examples: swimming, playing outside, or going to the beach.

Elephants in the Wild

Page 132: Sentences will vary. Examples of words: gray, big ears, long trunk, wrinkles.